实用雅思考试
写作模板

鸿儒英语教学教法研究所　编

中国水利水电出版社
www.waterpub.com.cn

内 容 提 要

本书在充分分析近几年雅思作文真题的基础上，按照议论文、应用文、图表作文的体裁，给出具有普遍适用性的固定句式和全文模板。基于雅思作文命题规律和趋势，按近年来雅思体裁和文体比例，最新预测15篇热点命题。每个预测皆给出推荐模板和范文。通过学习本书，能使读者在英语考试中规范写作思路，明确写作套路，节省考试时间，确保写作质量，从而切实提高作文成绩。

本书不仅可以作为雅思作文考试的参考用书，也可作为平时写作训练的指导用书。

图书在版编目（CIP）数据

一学就会的实用雅思考试写作模板 / 鸿儒英语教学教法研究所编. -- 北京 : 中国水利水电出版社, 2014.6
ISBN 978-7-5170-2083-7

Ⅰ. ①一… Ⅱ. ①鸿… Ⅲ. ①IELTS－写作－自学参考资料 Ⅳ. ①H315

中国版本图书馆CIP数据核字(2014)第118298号

书名	**一学就会的实用雅思考试写作模板**
作者	鸿儒英语教学教法研究所 编
出版发行	中国水利水电出版社 （北京市海淀区玉渊潭南路1号D座 100038） 网址：www. waterpub. com. cn E-mail：sales@waterpub. com. cn 电话：（010）68367658（发行部）
经售	北京科水图书销售中心（零售） 电话：（010）88383994、63202643、68545874 全国各地新华书店和相关出版物销售网点
排版	北京捷龙创易图文设计中心
印刷	北京嘉恒彩色印刷有限责任公司
规格	145mm×210mm 32开本 6印张 185千字
版次	2014年6月第1版 2014年6月第1次印刷
印数	0001—4000册
定价	**28.00**元

前言

一、不要盲目相信"作文模板"

英语写作是对英语语言技能综合运用的一种活动，它需要长期积累，并建立在相当程度的英语水平和个人修养之上。一部部名著、一篇篇精彩的文章看似洋洋洒洒，但都不是一蹴而就的，它要求作者有足够的词汇量和熟练的语法运用能力。而学习写作，首先要具备一定的阅读基础。所谓"读书破万卷，下笔如有神"就是这个道理。除此之外，还要努力实践，不能只是纸上谈兵。

谈到英语作文写作，很多人首先会想到"作文模板"。依靠一些适合开头、正文和结尾的固定句式，甚至是全文模板，的确能够在短时间内完成一篇文章，而通常这些固定句式是"高手"总结出来的，所以文章看上去也还算有一定质量。然而这种急功近利、临时抱佛脚的方法，绝不适合写作的学习。

二、"作文模板"只为应试而生

作为一种语言能力测试方式，英语应试作文考查的是学生的行文能力。只要作文内容符合主旨，逻辑合理，语法顺畅，语言得体，并适度地体现语言技能，得高分并非难事。由于英语考试的作文时间有限，如何在短时间内完成一定质量的文章，是有捷径可寻的。运用"作文模板"就是这样一条不适合写作学习，但却很适合应试写作的捷径。

三、本书的七大特色

本书立足应试，同时又帮助读者找到一条自由运用英语语言的道路。通过学习本书，读者可以在英语考试中规范写作思路、明确写作套路、节省考试时间、确保写作质量，从而切实提高作文成绩。具体来说，本书有以下几方面的特色。

提供作文的破题理念——全面概述各种英语考试的大纲要求，通过分析近十年来考试的真题作文，使考生洞悉命题规律，做到有针对性的复习。

提供丰富的句型模板——展示大量适用于文章开头、中间、结尾等不同语境的特色句型模板，丰富读者的句子库。

提供经典的全文模板——展示具有普遍适用性并具备基本承启和衔接语句的作文框架。

提供真题的记忆范文——记忆各种文体典型的真题范文，是作文应试的窍门。

提供全面的写作规范——所谓“细节决定成败”，掌握必要的写作规范，可让考生的作文“神形兼备”。

提供出彩的点睛之笔——写出打动阅卷者的点睛之笔是获得高分的关键，本书为读者精选了谚语格言、经典句式以及地道的英语搭配，让考生的作文更精彩。

精心预测，聚焦热点——基于雅思作文命题规律和命题趋势，按历年雅思作文体裁和文体比例，最新预测 15 篇热点命题。每个预测皆给出参考模板和范文。

我们希望考生在掌握这些作文模板并进行科学练习后，能够从容应对各种应试作文。也真诚地祝愿广大雅思考生在未来的考试中取得理想的成绩！

目录

第一章　解读雅思写作

第一节 关于雅思考试

雅思（International English Language Testing System，简称IELTS），与托福考试一样，也是一项国际英语水平测试，由剑桥大学测试中心、英国文化委员会和澳大利亚高校国际开发署共同管理。雅思考试分为两种模式：Academic（学术类），用于测试应试者的英语水平是否能够在英语环境中就读大学本科和研究生课程；General Training（普通培训类）则侧重评估应试者是否已具备在英语国家生存所需的基本英语技能，即Survival English。在欧洲和北美，越来越多的院校开始接受雅思考试成绩。英国、澳大利亚和新西兰等国的IELTS考试包括两类：

培训类（General Training）目前较多适用于移民。

学术类（Academic）目前较多适用于留学。

对中国考生来说，IELTS考试的词汇要求并不高，主要偏向生活化，因与TOEFL和国内英语考试（四六级）完全不同，所以掌握题型和快速解答就显得非常重要。

IELTS分为Listening、Reading、Writing和Speaking四个部分，每部分满分是9分，总分是四部分的平均值。

Listening：听力部分，时间为30分钟（另有10分钟写答案）；分4道大题，40个小题。

Reading：时间为60分钟，分为选择、填空、问答和匹配。

Writing：时间为60分钟。分为两个作文，第一个作文要求150个字，主要是描写数据、图表；第二个作文至少要写250个字，题材主要为议论文。

Speaking：时间为 10 ~ 15 分钟，进行一对一的考试方式。

IELTS 与 TOEFL、GRE、EPT 等考试的最大区别在于重在应用，不会专门考你的语法和词汇，考生很难靠短时间突击提高水平，关键在于日常积累。移民局将雅思考试成绩作为技术移民及其他类移民中衡量英语语言能力的唯一标准。

第二节 雅思考试写作概述与评分标准

一 雅思考试写作概述

雅思写作考试是继听力和阅读考试之后的第三部分，其目的是对考生英语书面交际能力的考核。时间为一个小时，要求考生完成两篇文章。培训类（General Training，简称 G 类）和学术类（Academic，简称 A 类）的写作任务 1（Task 1）不同，而写作任务 2（Task 2）相似。时间上的分配各有轻重，第一部分为 20 分钟，第二部分为 40 分钟。

写作任务 1（Task 1）——字数要求 150 字以上的文章

G 类写作要求考生根据题目要求写一封信，如投诉信、感谢信、道歉信、求职信、建议信、咨询信、邀请信、请求信等。其中以抱怨信和感谢信居多，或者是混合的信件，如某公司提供一个职称给你，你不能去，写信道歉并表示感谢。字数通常为 150 ~ 200 字（180 字左右为宜）。

A 类写作主要是测试考生总结和描述图表的能力。考生不用表达任何个人意见、评论、假设或结论。考试中出现的常规图表有线状图、柱状图、饼状图和表格，以柱状图和表格居多。有时是一种（个）图，有时是不同图表的组合，如线状图加饼状图，或表格加上柱状图等。偶尔会出现示意图，如地图、事物结构功能图、流程图或循环图等。其频率不高，基本上是平均一个季度考一次，以地图和流程图出现的几率较大。这类题型要求学生对一两幅由若干变化量组成的图表进行描述和比较，字数为150～200 字（180 字左右为宜）。

写作任务 2（Task 2）——字数要求至少 250 字的文章

A 类和 G 类写作在 Task 2 方面极为相似，经常出现 G 类作文曾经是 A 类作文题目的现象。Task 2 是写一篇议论文或说明文，A 类通常考试议论文，而 G 类说明文居多。字数以 280 字左右为宜。

该任务要求考生根据题目进行论证，表明态度或作出描述。也就是说，对一组相对的观点进行讨论（Discuss both sides/views and give your opinion. Does this trend bring more positive or negative effects to the society?）。例如，有人认为老师应该负责教学生辨认是非、行为规范，而另一些人认为老师只教学生理论知识就可以了，要求讨论双方并表明自己的观点。或是要求对某个观点发表支持或反对意见（Do you agree or disagree?To what extent do you agree or disagree?），例如，有人认为市民应该留住自己赚的所有钱而不应该纳锐，你同不同意？又或是解释某种现象带来的问题，分析其原因并提出解决办法等（What problems will the youth unemployment cuuse to individuals and the society? Give reasons and make some suggestions.）。例如，青少年吸毒由什么原因引起，会带来什么问题，提出解决办法等。

二 雅思考试写作评分标准

从 2007 年 7 月 1 日开始，雅思写作的评分标准出现了一个小变化，也就是雅思写作跟阅读和听力一样，也有半分制。

（一）书信或图表评分标准

1. TA（Task Achievement）任务完成情况

最简单的理解是所写文章是否覆盖了题目要求的所有任务，也就是是否完成了题目里面的所有指令。具体来说，题目里所有的要点，必须一一覆盖，缺一不可，同时，所写的内容必须符合情理经得起推敲。图表写作应该对图表进行一到两句总的概述，并选择相应的数据进行支持。所以考生不能罗列里面所有的数据，而是对有意义的数据进行重点描述。

2. C. C（Coherence and Cohesion）连贯性和统一性

这里主要指的是行文过程里面如何通过一些手段加强连接，实现文章的上下连贯，加强文章的流畅性。G 类小作文的衔接手段通常由有逻辑、语法和语义关系的连接词充当。A 类小作文更多通过表示逻辑的连接词或套句进行连接。

3. LR（Lexical Resource）词汇资源

词汇资源，主要是指评估词的多样化（variety）。通常来说，他们是通过同义词的替换和词性的变化达成的。写作的过程要尽量避免同一个单词不断出现，不然，考官会觉得这个考生的词汇很有限。另外，还从词的使用频率上面评估（less common），也就是词的深度了。一般来说，我们可以通过词缀变化达到目标。例如，not responsible 可以用 irresponsible 来代替，该词使用频率较低。

4. GRA（Grammatical Range and Accuracy）语法应用范围和准确率

语法应用范围是指句式的变化，也就是在文章中考生掌握句子结构的范围，如 6 分的文章必须出现复杂的结构，包括分词结构和复合句。准确性主要反映在句子的完整度、主谓一致、名词单复数、定冠词的使用、单词是否正确以及标点符号的使用等方面。

（二）议论文或说明文评分标准

1. TR（Task Response）任务反馈情况

考生一定要记住完成作文要求的各项任务，遗漏了任何任务都会导致失分，从而影响文章的总体得分。例如，有些考生把 Discuss both sides and give your opinion 写成了只讨论一边的观点。遗漏任务还包括字数不足、表达不清楚、问题不明确、建议不及时等。同时，偏题或跑题也是很严重的问题，如有些学生把 automobile 看作 mobile phones，这样写出来的文章就不知所云了。所以，考生在审题的时候就要特别注意。另外，任务的反馈还包括段落的布局、分段是否合理、是否对观点进行充分的论证，还有论点是否深刻等。

2. C. C（Coherence and Cohesion）连贯性和统一性

统一性指的是文章的前后照应，例如引言段表了态，结尾段就重申观点，相反，如果引言段没有表态，结尾段就表态。又如，论点要能论证观点，论据要围绕论点展开。连贯性则包括句子之间的连贯，论点之间的连贯和段落之间的连贯等，通常是通过有逻辑关系的连接词完成的。

3. LR（Lexical Resource）词汇资源

词汇资源是考察考生词汇的多样化和对使用频率不高的词汇的把握，从考生词汇的宽度和深度进行评判。多样化主要是同义词的互换，特别要指出的是，同义词的互换并不是简单的一个词跟另一个词的替换，可以通过单词、词组、甚至从句进行。例如，失业的年轻人可以说是 the unemployed youth，the jobless young people，young people who stay jobless，young people without work/jobs，the youth joblessness 等。词的深度主要是评估考生对少用的词汇是否能正确把握使用。如“有害的”，一般考生会用 harmful，但 damaging 或 detrimental 就更有深度了，甚至还可以用到动词 impair。

4. GRA（Grammatical Range and Accuracy）语法应用范围和准确率

句式的变化要做到多样化。高分的文章，通常以长句为主，辅以短句。例如，7 分的文章里面，除了要有 6 分的复杂结构，还要求做到并列句、综合句、强调句、倒装句、虚拟语气、双重否定句、比较句式，甚至标点符号的使用等。同时，正确使用被动语态也很重要，尤其是一些高分的被动时态语态。如现在完成时被动、现在进行时的被动等。

（三）雅思 Task 1 各个档次具体评分标准

	完成任务	连贯和衔接	词汇和资源	语法结构的范围和准确性
9 分作文	完全满足写作的所有要求	分段合理，不露痕迹地使用衔接手段	使用广泛，很少出现错误	语法结构使用广泛、准确
8 分作文	充分涵盖题目的所有要求，观点明确，论证充分	分段充分、适当，衔接词运用得得体；观点明确有逻辑	能流畅地使用各种词汇来表达观点；能巧妙地使用不常见的词语和词组，尽管搭配和选词上有不当；拼写和构词错误少	灵活地使用多种结构，大部分的语句都是正确的
7 分作文	覆盖题目的要求，文章思路清晰，语气一贯、得体，清晰呈现出核心信息，但还可以更加充分扩展	信息观点组织具有逻辑性、延续性；衔接手段使用合理，虽然可能有些使用过多或过少	词汇使用丰富，能使用较不常见的词汇；拼写和语法上偶尔有错误	使用多种复杂结构，大部分语句无误；语法和标点掌握较好，但可能会犯一些错误

续表

	完成任务	连贯和衔接	词汇和资源	语法结构的范围和准确性
6分作文	回应题目的要求，立场明确，虽然结论不清晰或重复，主要观点切题，但有观点可能论证不够充分或清晰	文章有延续性，信息和观点组织连贯；衔接手段使用有效，但句子之间衔接可能会不准确；指代关系不能合理地使用	使用适当范围内的词汇；在使用较不常见的词汇时不准确，拼写、构词法上有错误，但是不影响交际	使用简单的复杂句结构；语法标点出现一些错误
5分作文	只是部分回应题目的要求，格式可能有时不准确；有立场，但是发展部分不清晰，有主要观点，但有限且不充分或存在不相关的细节	有一定的组织，但是缺少总体的延续性；衔接手段不准确或过度使用，缺少指代或替换；没有分段，或分段不充分	使用有限的词汇量；拼写和构词法上可能出现明显的错误	使用基本句子结构，使用复杂句有错误；语法标点错误很多
4分作文	在最低限度上完成任务或者文章离题；格式不得体；立场不清晰，有的部分表意不明、重复或者错误	提供了信息和观点，但安排不连贯；使用基本的衔接手法，但是不准确或者重复；没有分段	使用基本的词汇，可能重复或不得体；构词法和拼写掌握有限，理解困难	从句很少看见，有的结构准确但是错误很多；标点错误

续表

	完成任务	连贯和衔接	词汇和资源	语法结构的范围和准确性
3分作文	没有充分回应文章的要求，没有清晰的立场，观点有限，并且很不充分	文章没有逻辑性；衔接手段也使用得非常有限；不能充分表明自己的观点	错误严重干扰信息的传递；表达、构词法有限	语法、标点还有拼写错误很多
2分作文	内容和要求几乎无关	对各个段落组织得不合理	词汇量少；没有基本的语法和拼写基础	词汇使用极其有限，除了背诵的短语以外无法使用句子
1分作文	内容和要求无关	无法交流信息	只有一些比较散的单词	完全无法使用句子
0分作文	缺席考试，交白卷，完全抄袭背诵好的范文			

第二章　雅思各类体裁作文模板

第一节 议论文模板

一 分解句型模板

✲ 常用开头模板

1. A recent newspaper article reveals that…
最近报纸上的文章上揭露了……
2. Many people applaud/welcome this new development while others have expressed their concern about this.
很多人赞同/欢迎这个新趋势，而另外一些人对这个趋势有他们自己的看法。
3. Everyone wants to be…, …has become much more popular.
每个人都想……，……已经很受欢迎。
4. The benefits of…are numerous; it is especially beneficial for…
……的好处有很多；它对……尤其有利。
5. Some think that…That is to say, …
一些人认为……也就意味着……
6. The opening policy means that…
这个开放的政策意味着……
7. Instead of…tends to…because of…
而不是/相反……倾向……因为……
8. It seemed (outrageous) for me to…that…
令我（不能容忍的）是……
9. …will surely consider…Yet I have my reasons.
……很确信地认为……而我有我的理由。

10. Now an increasing number of people come to realize that…
现在开始有越来越多的人意识到……
11. That has become the most important criterion for…
那已经变成衡量……最重要的标准。
12. In the past few years, quite a number of…have chosen to…
在过去的几年里，有相当一部分……选择了……
13. Nowadays, one phenomenon calls for people's attention that…
如今，一个现象引起了人们的注意，即……
14. …becoming more and more intolerable because of…
……变得让人越来越无法忍受，是因为……
15. …are the typical examples that…Besides, …
……是典型的例子。另外，……
16. If you … what will you feel? Of course, you will feel … because…
如果你……你会有什么感觉呢？当然，你会觉得……因为……
17. We must recognize that…Once…it is wise to…
我们必须认识到……一旦……就会（让）……知道。
18. Most of us today recognize that …, … has been a greatly serious problem. Therefore, …
今天我们很多人认识到……，……已经成为很严重的问题。所以……
19. In contemporary society, …has become a serious problem in our country, and it is not extremely astonishing for us to…
在当代社会，在我们国家……已经成为一个很重要的问题，……（现象）令我们不是很吃惊。
20. Under such circumstances, these phenomena have already aroused public concern.
在这样的环境下，这些现象已经引起了公众的关注。

21. Despite various improvements in all aspects of...
尽管在……（上/所有方面）有很多进展。
22. As...in China, ...has become one of the most momentous problems which every big city is confronted with.
就像……在中国，……已经成为每个大城市要面临的非常重要的问题之一。
23. To seek a better way out of the present straits, city planners have come up with...
为了找到解决困境的方法，城市规划者提出……
24. In our society, ...is still regarded as the most important...
在我们的社会上，……始终被看作一个重要的……
25. With the further development of the reform of ..., it is necessary for us to...
随着……改革的进一步完善，……对我们来说是很有必要的。
26. With the development of..., ...are involved in it. But when it comes to...there are different opinions.
随着……的发展，……涉及其中，但是，当……的时候，有很多不同的观点。
27. Nowadays, ...has become more and more popular in China. A growing number of people in China are immersed in...
现在，……在中国已经很流行。很多中国人陷入……
28. When it comes to the necessity of...views vary from person to person.
当……变得有必要时，不同的人有不同的观点。
29. Now it is common to...There is no consensus of opinions among people as to the view of it.
现在，……是很正常的。对于这个观点，人们没有达成一致的看法。
30. With the reform and opening-up policy being carried out,

thousands upon thousands of…are crowding into…

随着改革开放政策的实施，成千上万的……开始涌入……

31. …is becoming more and more popular and it has got into people's life.

……变得越来越受欢迎，同时也走进了人们的生活。

32. In China, more and more cases of…are frequently reported in recent years.

在中国，近几年出现越来越多关于……的频繁报道。

33. Some people take it for granted that…In their mind, … Besides…

一些人认为……是理所当然的。他们认为……，另外……

34. When asked about … different people will offer different opinions.

每当被问起……，每个人都有不同的观点。

35. …finally succeeded in…after many efforts. …will influence …greatly…

……终于在不断的努力下取得了在……（上）的成功，……会在……上产生深远影响。

36. Nowadays, …may come across the…

现今，……遇到了……问题。

37. …have founded their way into a wide area of every life. Obviously it is very convenient in people's daily life.

……已经深入到日常生活中的众多领域。很明显的，它在人们的日常生活中很便利。

38. …have created a lot of serious problems. Besides, …are responsible for a good part of…

……已经产生很多严重的问题，另外，……应该对……负一部分责任。

39. The recent years have witnessed an unfavorable social phenomenon…

近几年来出现了一种不好的社会现象……

40. From the resent news, we learn that nowadays ... For example, ...
从最近的新闻来看，我们了解到近来……。例如……

41. In addition, man is faced with problems of...As a result, how to resolve it is worth paying attention to.
另外，人类面临着的问题是……。所以，如何来解决这个问题很值得我们去关注。

42. Despite various improvements in all aspects of...
尽管在……上出现了很多进步。

43. There has been a discussion recently about...It is obviously that...So...is worth paying attention to.
最近出现了一些关于……的争论。很明显……。所以……是值得关注的。

44. ...has long been a custom for...However, these years the Chinese people have different opinions about...
……已经成为了……的一种习惯。然而，最近这几年中国人对……产生了不同的观点。

45. Entering the 21st century, ...is now in an age of...plays an increasingly important role and all people have to...
进入21世纪，在……的年代，……起着越来越重要的作用，所有人不得不……

46. Many people believe that...the truth is deep and profound. As we know, ...
很多人相信……，这个事实的意义很深远，如我们所知……

47. There is no complete argument among people as to...
关于……的（观点或者辩论）中，没有一个人可以提出完整的论据（或者论点）。

48. Recently the phenomenon has become a heated topic.

最近这个现象已经成为一个很热的话题。

49. There is in fact one reason for us to believe that…

有一个让我们信服的事实是……

50. Recently the issue has aroused great concern among…

最近，这个话题在……中引起了很大的关注。

51. Nowadays there is a growing concern over…

现在，对……的关注持续升温。

52. Currently there is a widespread concern that…

最近，一个很普遍的焦点是……

53. These days we are often told that…, but is this really the case?

最近，我们经常得知……，但是这是真正的情况吗？

54. With the development of the society, more and more people enroll in…

随着社会的发展，越来越多的人涌入……

55. …has been one medium of…that has connected all the people around world. More and more people tend to concern the…

……已经成了一种……的媒介，同时它还将世界各地的人连接在一起。越来越多的人关注……

56. In this essay, I will investigate my own opinion of it.

在这篇文章中，我会具体陈述我的观点。

57. To tackle these problems, …would seem helpful.

为了解决这些问题，……看起来很有帮助。

58. As our society has entered the information age and commercialization is sweeping across the world.

由于我们的社会已经进入信息时代，商品化正在风靡全球。

59. It is commonly recognized that…play a large role in advancement of our society.

我们普遍认识到……在我们社会前进的道路上起着重要的

作用。

60. In principle, however, I side with…
总体而言，我支持……

61. One of the most challenging problems of today's society is…
当今社会中，最富有挑战性的问题之一是……

62. To seek a better way out of the present straits, many proposals have been put forward to solve this problem.
为了寻求一个更好的解决现在困境的方法，有很多解决这个问题的建议已经提出。

63. Different people hold different ideas on this practice. Personally, I think there are some valid reasons in this argument.
在这个问题上每个人都持有不同的看法。我个人认为这些争论都有自己的理由。

64. Nowadays, …are thorny issues in every major city all around the world.
现在，……在世界的每个主要城市都成了很棘手的问题。

65. Nevertheless, I am thoroughly in support of above statement and will endeavor to exemplify my opinion on this matter throughout the following discussion.
然而，我完全支持以上论述并将通过以下讨论来举例说明我对这个问题的看法。

66. A prevailing phenomenon nowadays is that …, which are becoming more and more assimilated.
……成为现如今很普遍的一种现象，并越来越被同化了。

67. Therefore, there arises a fierce debate concerning the proposal that…
因此，对于这个提议产生了激烈的争论……

68. One's attitude towards…would largely depend on…
一个人关于……的观点在一定程度上是取决于……

✲ 常用主体内容模板

1. People who…have their reasons. Some people are in favor of the idea. First, they think that…Second, …That is to say… Third, …

   那些……的人们有着他们的理由。一些人支持这个观点。第一，他们认为……。第二，……。也就是说……。第三，……

2. A major of people consider it very important to hold… They agree that… However, …

   大部分人认为支持……（的观点）是很重要的。他们同意……。可是……

3. There are a variety of aspects contributing to this trend. First, …For example, … Second, with the development of economy, …

   有很多支持这个观点（趋势）的因素。第一……。例如……。第二，……随着经济的发展……

4. Some people maintain that … Some people maintain that … Meanwhile, as is well-known, a person's energy is limited. So, …

   一些人坚持……。一些人坚持……。同时，就我们所知，一个人的精力是有限的，所以……

5. We like…because we can benefit from it. It certainly…

   我们喜欢……因为我们能从中得到很多好处。当然……

6. In my opinion, I think…such as…As a result, they will…

   在我看来，我认为……例如……。所以，他们会……

7. …not only…but…Besides… Generally speaking…

   ……不仅……而且……。此外……。一般来说……

8. In many large cities, … And furthermore, … But this solution…Compared with other solution, …

   在很多大城市，……。而且，……。但是这个解决方法……。与其他的方法相比……

9. What should we do to…? There are many ways which help to…
关于……我们该怎么做呢？对于帮助……有很多方法。
10. Nowadays in China…With the appearance of all kinds of…
现在在中国……。随着各种……的出现……
11. There are a quite number of factors, and the main reason is the…
有许多的因素，主要的原因是……
12. From above, we can find that the reasons why … are as follows. The primary reason, I think, … For example, … However, … Second, … The third reason actually is the result of…
从以上论述我们可以发现……的原因如下，主要的原因，我想是……。例如，……。然而，……。第二，……。第三个原因实际上是……的结果。
13. To…we should first… Let's take…as an example. Besides… It can result in…
为了……我们应该先……。让我们以……为例。此外……。它可以导致……
14. To…we should also… Again let's take…as an example. So it is impossible to…
为了……我们同样也要……。让我再一次以……为例。所以……是不可能的。
15. No easy solution can be taken to cope with the problem of…, but… Therefore, my viewpoint is that…
没有一个容易的方法来解决……（问题），只有……。因此我的观点是……
16. Serious as the problem seems, we can come up with some measures to deal with it.
问题正如我们所见的严重，我们能提出很多方法来解决它。
17. I think that… It is of great importance…

我认为……。……是很重要的。

18. For one thing, … (For example…) For another, …
一方面……(例如……)。另一方面……

19. In fact, however, … Above all… Furthermore, …
事实上，尽管如此，……。总之……。进一步来说，……

20. There are many advantages/disadvantages of this modern way.
这种现代做法存在很多优点/缺点。

21. But in the process of opening to the outside, some negative factors will inevitably occur. Therefore, …
但是在对外开放的过程中，必然产生一些负面的因素。因此，……

22. Others advocate…That is to say, no matter…
其他人提倡……。也就是说，不管……

23. People today are… To avoid…we should… However, … If not done properly, … If overdone, it can…
今天的人们……。为了避免……我们应该……。然而……。如果做得不合理……。如果过度，它能……

24. Those who take sides against this new trend believe that… because…
那些反对新趋势的人们相信……因为……

25. One common argument, however, for…, …is that…
然而，一个普遍论据是……，因为……，……是……

26. In most cities, …has been taking shape.
在大多数城市，……已经发展得很具规模。

27. The solutions to this problem seem more than clear on this occasion. To create more job opportunities, … Moreover, … Last but by no means the least, …
解决这个问题的办法看起来很明确。为了创造更多的就业机会，……，而且……。最后……

28. It should be paid attention to that…On one hand, … On the other hand, … Therefore, it is high time that…
更值得关注的是……。一方面……。另一方面……。因此，正是……的时候。
29. Many people applaud it and argue that… They think…
很多人赞同它并且争论到……。他们认为……
30. However, …, for example that…And it is possible that…
然而，……，例如……。并且它很可能……
31. Many people…, mainly for two reasons. In most cases, …
很多人……，大体上有两种原因。在大多数情况下，……
32. Some people think that…is a good thing. In their eyes, …
一些人认为……是一件好事情。在他们的眼里……
33. However, others think that… The result, sometimes, is that…
然而，其他人认为……。结果，有时是……
34. Others, on the other hand, … The main reasons are that…but also may cause troubles. For example, …
其他人，从另一方面来讲……。主要的原因是……但是同样会带来问题。例如……
35. However, …, for example that…And it is possible that…
然而……，例如……。并且它很可能……
36. Personally, I am in favor of the former opinion.
就我个人而言，我很赞成之前的观点。
37. Many remarkable reasons contribute to this argument. First of all, … For example, …
很多显著的理由都可以支持这个论据。首先，……。例如……
38. The main reason why people … is, perhaps, for … For example, …
人们为什么……的主要原因，可能是……。例如，……
39. First, it is the demand of…That is why… Second, it is well-

known that…

第一，这是……的需要。这就是为什么……。第二，众所周知……

40. In my opinion, I think this question should be probed in depth. On one hand, the first group is not totally correct because… On the other hand, the second group seems… because…

在我看来，我认为这个问题应该更透彻地去讨论。一方面，第一组并不完全正确是因为……。另一方面，第二组看起来……因为……

41. However, the changes of environment have caused quite a number of harmful effects.

然而，环境的改变带来了很多不好的影响。

42. A number of factors could account for the development in…

有很多因素能够说明在……上发展的原因。

43. It is not simple to give the reason for this complicated phenomenon…

对于……这个复杂的现象，很难给出一个合理的原因。

44. There are several causes for this significant growth in…, first…, second…, finally…

关于……的不断上涨，存在着很多原因，第一……，第二……，最后……

45. Among the most convincing reasons given, one should be mentioned…

从上述最重要的理由中，我们可以提出……

46. Besides, we should not neglect that…

另外，我们不应该忽视……

47. Yet differences will be found. That's why I feel that…

这些差异已经找到了，这也是为什么我觉得……（的原因）。

48. But/However, have you noticed…? But this is not whole… Some of…
但是/然而，你有没有注意到……？但是它不是全部……。一些……
49. There are numerous examples supporting this argument. A case in point is that…
有无数的例子证明这个论据，其中一个恰当的例子是……
50. (Most) people consider… In fact, they will choose…
（大部分）人认为……。事实上，他们会选择……
51. However, …, have terrible side effects. What's worse, …
然而，……，有很坏的副作用。更严重的是……
52. On the contrary, … come up with many novel ideas countering the opinions mentioned above.
相反，……提出很多新的想法来反对以上提到的看法。
53. The most immediate reason for it being difficult for us to…
最直接的原因对我们来说很难……
54. There are quite number of occasions on which we have to…
有很多情况使我们不得不……
55. Some people hold that the principle reason for these problems lies with…
一些人们坚持这些问题的主要原因在于……
56. Statistics in…indicate that…
关于……的统计数字表明了……
57. Proponents of the former view believe that…
支持前者的人相信……
58. Opponents of this view argue that…
反对这个观点的人争论道……
59. Others insist that there are undoubtedly some disadvantages of…
另外一些人坚持，……毫无疑问有很多缺点。

60. However, everything has two sides…gives rise to a number of problems.
然而，任何事情都有两面，……引起了很多问题。
61. Besides, it is even more debatable to…
另外，变得越来越争议的是……
62. However, the choice varies from person to person.
然而，不同的人有不同的选择。
63. In my opinion, this serious issue is as indication of…
在我看来，这个严重的问题是……的象征。
64. As different people have different understanding on the…, there are bound to be perennial discussions of the pros and cons of growing.
如同不同的人对于……有着不同的理解，也必然将正反两方面意见继续讨论下去。
65. By way of forming my own opinion to the assigned statement, I will discuss the many virtues of…
通过形成我对已提出论述的观点，我会讨论关于……的一些优点。
66. The previous two arguments are based on…
之前的两种争论是以……为根据的。
67. Different reasons can be identified as contributing to this situation. The following reasons my view on…
不同的原因可以被认为导致出现这种状况，以下原因是我对……的看法。

✲ 常用结尾模板

1. Of the two views discussed above, I'm in favor of the…
上述讨论的两种观点，我更倾向于……
2. In short, if done correctly, … It will become an important part of our life.
总之，如果实施合理，……。它将成为我们生命中很重要的一部分。

3. In a word, with the…increasing popularity of…
   总之，随着……的不断普及。
4. Taking my experience into account, I draw the conclusion that…
   考虑到我自己的经验，我得出的结论为……
5. What I said above does not mean that…
   我上面所要表达的不是……
6. …is a natural part of everyday life. What we can do is to…
   ……是我们生活中常见的一部分。我们可以做的是……
7. As far as I am concerned, … In a word, …
   在我看来……。总之……
8. In view of all this, …Firstly, …Secondly, …(Thirdly, …) And finally, …
   考虑到所有这些，……。第一，……。第二，……。（第三，……。）最后……
9. There is no doubt that…
   毫无疑问……
10. However, no matter how difficult it is, we should… In fact… Once…, we should… Instead, we should…
    然而，不管这个问题有多困难，我们应该……。事实上……。一旦……，我们应该……。相反我们应该……
11. Therefore, …moreover, … Let's make our good efforts
    因此，……然而……。让我们做出我们的努力……
12. From my perspective, it is imperative for us to implement effective and efficient measures to … For one thing … For another thing, …
    从我的角度来看，我们很有必要来实施有效的且高效的方法来……。首先……，其次……
13. In order to…both parts should…What they shouldn't do…
    为了……两者都应该……。我们不应该……

14. The significance of the…First, … Besides, … it also… For instance, … Meanwhile, …
（关于）……的重要性。首先，……。此外，……同样的……。例如，……。同时，……
15. But other people don't think like that because … For instance, … In a word, …
但是其他的人不这样认为因为……。例如，……。总之，……
16. The necessity of… Therefore, there is no doubt that we should…
（关于）……的必要性……。因此，毋庸质疑我们应该……
17. Judging from the above, … Certainly, there is little doubt that further attention will be paid to this issue.
根据以上的判断，……。当然，我们毫无疑问要对这件事加倍关注。
18. The solutions to the problem are difficult to…
问题的解决方法很难……
19. From now on, …is more pressing than ever before.
从现在开始，……已经变得比以前更加紧迫。
20. Personally, I side with the former opinion. Because…
依我自己看，我支持前面的观点。因为……
21. In my opinion, everyone should put the right attitude to…
在我看来，每个人对……都应该有个正确的态度。
22. None of the solutions is quite satisfactory. The problem should be examined in a new way.
没有一个解决方法值得满意。这个问题需要用新的方法来解决。
23. Thus, this is the reason why we must…
因此，这是我们为什么必须……的原因。
24. On account of this we can find that…
由于这个我们可以发现……

25. Therefore, these findings reveal the following information...
因此，这些发现揭示了以下的信息……
26. The result is dependent on...
这个结果是根据……
27. It is high time that we put considerable emphasis on...
是我们该重点强调……的时候了。
28. We might do more than identify the cause. It is important to take actions to...
我们可以在找出原因上做的更多；采取……的行动很重要。
29. It is high time that strict measures were taken to stop...
是该采取准确的方法来阻止……了。
30. Taking all these into account, we...
考虑到所有的问题，我们……
31. With the efforts of all parts concerned, the problem will be solved thoroughly.
随着所有方面的努力，问题将被彻底地解决。
32. There is no easy method, but...might be of some help.
没有比较轻松的办法，但是……可能会有一些帮助。
33. It is necessary that steps should be taken to...
有必要采取……措施。
34. To solve the above-mentioned problem, we must...
为了解决以上的问题，我们应该……
35. In summary, if we continue to ignore the above-mentioned issue, more problems will crop up.
总之，如果我们继续忽视以上的问题，更多的问题就会接踵而来。
36. Whether it is good or not/positive or negative, one thing is certain/clear...
不管是好还是坏/有积极的或者消极的影响，很肯定的是……

37. In order to…both parts should…What they shouldn't do…
为了……，两方面都应该……。他们不应该做的是……
38. The solutions vary according to different situations, therefore the problem of…remains far from being solved.
解决的方法根据不同的情形而定，因此，……的问题还远远没有解决。
39. As long as…make joint efforts, a sound solution is not far away.
只要……取得了合作的效果，一个有效的解决办法就将会出现。
40. It is quite natural that we meet such problems along the route of…
我们遇到关于……的问题是很正常的现象。
41. A suggestion is made to… People should be…
建议……。人们应该……
42. First of all, as for me, … This is because the … Secondly, …Thirdly, … Only in this way can we…
首先，对于我来说，……。那是因为……。第二，……。第三，……。只有这样我们才能……
43. The decision … makes about … will undoubtedly have tremendous influence on society.
……的决定使得……会毫无疑问地对我们的社会产生巨大的影响。
44. As far as I am concerned, the question is not…but…
我认为，这个问题不是……而是……
45. Only in this way can we achieve success and meet the needs of ourselves as well as the society.
只有这样我们才能成功并且能满足我们自己和这个社会。
46. Taking the above-mentioned factors into consideration, I may reasonable conclude that…

考虑到以上所有的因素，我可以很合理地得出……

47. In fact, more than three ways can be adopted. As for me, I prefer to…
事实上，有多于三种的方法可以被采用。对于我，我更倾向于……

48. In my opinion, there are many reasons for my choice. The main reason is that…
在我看来，我的选择有很多原因。最主要的原因是……

49. In a word, we can see clearly that the key lies in…
总之，我们很明显地了解到关键在于……

50. When all the factors are discussed, we may safely come to the conclusion that…
讨论过所有因素后，我们可以得到的结论是……

51. In fact, I must admit that…
事实上，我必须承认……

52. Taking the above-mentioned factors into consideration, I may reasonably conclude that…
考虑到以上的因素，我可以合理地作结论……

53. However, …also create some problems. Therefore, we have a long way to go to solve the problem.
然而，……同样出现很多问题。因此，我们有很长的时间去解决这个问题。

54. We must try our best to find new beneficial ways to…
我们必须竭尽全力去发现新的有利的方法来……

55. It may bring about/produce/cause a considerable change in… This will bring some serious dreadful consequence.
它会引起在……上的巨大的转变。这会带来很多致命的后果。

56. Both governments and ordinary citizens should join hands to make this world a better place to live in, not only for

ourselves, but also for future generations.
政府和百姓应该携手并肩共创一个更好的生活环境，不仅仅是为了我们自己，同样是为了我们的后代。

57. We must look for/search for/call for an immediate solution/action/method/measure because the present/current situation/state of... If permitted to continue, it will surely/certainly lead to/result in the destruction/the end of...
我们必须寻找一个直接的方法，因为现在的形势是……。如果这样肆意下去，必然会导致……的破坏。

58. Obviously/Clearly/Apparently/No doubt that there is very little chance that... unless there is an immediate action of/common realization of...
显然地，我们只有很小的机会……除非有一个直接的方法/共同的认识……

二 背诵经典全文模板

（一）个人观点议论文

模板 1

Nowadays more and more people pay more attention on ________. Some people argue that ________ in that ________, while others firmly hold that ________.

In my opinion, I think this question should be probed in depth. On one hand, the first group is not totally correct because ________.

On the other hand, the second group seems ________ because ________.

In a word, we can see clearly that the key lies in ________. Otherwise ________.

分析： 开门见山，直接提出观点，强调一部分人的观点和另一部分的观点
表明自己的观点，一部分人观点
另一部分人的观点和原因
总结全文，指出正确的观点

模板 2

When asked about ________, different people will offer different opinions. Some people take it for granted that ________. In their mind, ________. Besides, ________.
However, others hold that ________. They maintain that ________, and ________.
Weighing up these two arguments, I am for the first one.
For one thing, ________.
For another, ________. For instance, ________.
Therefore, as stated above, ________.

分析： 开门见山，直接进入主题，表明不同的人有不同的观点，一部分人的观点
转折，指出另一部分人的看法和原因
综合所有的观点，提出自己的看法，举例具体说明原因

模板 3

Upon ________, ________ will face with ________, that is, ________.
However, the choice varies from person to person. Some ________.
Some ________. Also, ________.
As to me, ________.

In my opinion, there are many reasons for my choice. The main reason is that ________. So in my heart, ________. In addition, ________.

分析：说明我们要面临的问题
一些人的选择
另一些人的选择
我的选择
我的看法和理由

模板 4

Now an increasing number of people come to realize that ________.

However, personally I think that ________ has become the most important criterion for ________. From one thing ________.

From another thing, ________. What's more, ________. As a result, ________.

分析：问题的出现
我的看法，从一方面进行阐述说明
从另一方面来说明影响
结果

模板 5

It becomes a common tendency these days for people to ________. Many people are opposed/agreed to ________ because they think ________.

They often argued that ________.

In my mind, however, I can't agree with ________. At the same time, ________. In addition, ________.

In conclusion, ________.

分析： 直接引出观点，说明不同的人持有不同的观点并指出原因

进一步阐明大家的观点

提出自己看法并进一步阐明

总结

模板 6

A criticism often heard these days is that ________. They say that ________.

I disagree/agree with the point of view for ________.

My first reason is that ________.

My second reason is that ________.

My third reason is based on ________.

All is all, ________.

分析： 引出评论的出现和一些人的看法

我的观点

我的第一个理由

第二个理由

第三个理由

总结

模板 7

There is a growing tendency these days for people to discuss ________. In this essay, I will investigate my own opinion of it.

On the one hand, ________, for example, ________.

On the other hand, ________. However, ________.

All in all, ________.

分析： 交代了问题的出现给人们带来的影响，我的态度

具体说明产生这一现象的原因，从一方面进一步阐述（举例子）
从另一方面阐述
总结我的观点

模板 8

It is not uncommon these days/years for ________. In my opinion, this increasingly common and serious issue is as indication of ________.

Some of ________, for examples, ________. To tackle these problems, ________ would seem helpful.

In addition, ________.

On the other hand, ________. As a consequence, ________.

In a word, ________.

分析： 说明问题的出现和我的看法
举例说明
进一步解释说明
从另一个角度分析
总结

模板 9

There is a growing tendency nowadays for ________. This lead to ________. Yet, in my opinion, ________.

It is an undeniable face that ________. Therefore, to some extent, ________.

There is no doubt that ________.

To sum up, ________.

分析： 说明问题的出现和带来的影响，以及我的态度

强调并解释这个现象的出现带来的影响
进一步说明
总结

模板 10

These days there is a growing tendency for ________ to have difficulties in ________. A large number of people hold the opinion that ________. ________. For my part, I am in favor of ________.

In the first place, ________ is demanded by our ever-developing society. As our society has entered the information age and commercialization is sweeping across the world, ________.

In the second place, ________.

When all the factors are discussed we may safely come to the conclusion that ________.

分析： 直接说明问题的出现给人们带来的影响，不同人的观点和我的态度
从一方面说明原因
从另一方面说明
总结

模板 11

For the past several decades, ________ has been at the center of heated debate from ________. Often times, ________. In this essay, I will investigate some ________. However, ________.

In fact, ________. Research has shown that ________.

Researchers are also concerned that ________.

In addition to the points raised above, ________.

分析： 交代了问题早在以前就开始出现，我针对这个现象提出自己的一些看法
举例说明
进一步说明原因
综上所述，给出自己的结论

模板 12

More and more people pay more attention to ________, which not only ________, but also ________. Therefore, ________.

As we all know, ________ is closely related to many things, such as ________. With the growing popularity of ________, more and more people begin to choose that for ________.

In the second place, ________.

In summary, as far as I am concerned, ________. As a result, ________.

分析： 提出问题，说明人们关注的原因
具体说明导致问题出现的原因
从另一角度说明
总结，我的看法

模板 13

In the recent days, there is a growing popularity of ________. An increasing number of ________, and ________ has become one of the most important part in their daily life.

________ has attracted ________ was related to the following reasons. On the one hand ________.

On the other hand, ________, for example, ________. However, ________.

In my mind, ________, we can say that ________. If you want to ________, you had better ________. All in all, ________.

分析： 开门见山，直接提出主题及影响

从一方面解释说明问题出现的原因

从另一方面举例子说明

转折强调

我的观点和看法

模 板 14

It is commonly recognized that ________ play a large role in advancement of our society. ________, however, ________.

It can be argued that ________. In addition, ________. Besides, ________. For instance, ________. Therefore, ________.

From another point, we can see that ________.

In summary, in comparison, ________.

分析： 问题的出现及其影响

大家对这个问题的评论

进一步具体说明

从另外一个方面说明

在相比之下得出结论

模 板 15

With the fast development of urbanization, ________. But others argue that ________. In principle, however, I side with

________.

In the first point, to some degree, ________.

In the second point, ________.

In the third point, ________.

As mentioned above, I can draw a conclusion that it is necessary to ________.

分析： 随着社会的发展，很多人会争论到的问题，我的看法

从第一个方面来说明

第二个方面

第三个方面

总结概括

经典范例

Directions: *Some people think that the government should provide assistance to all kinds of artists includes painters, musicians, poets, however, other people think that is a waste of money for providing this assistance. State your opinion.*

There is a growing tendency these days for many people to discuss whether the government should provide assistance to all kinds' of artists. To be of assistance or not, it indeed is debatable if artists deserve and require funding by the government. In this essay, I will investigate my own opinion of it.

On the one hand, I acknowledge that the benefits from artists and poets can enrich our everyday lives in so many different ways, for example, their works of arts could cultivate people's taste and make people have a good mood. Otherwise we cannot imagine our life without them, maybe only become a lot tedious.

On the other hand, there is a large group of artists is neither rich nor famous, they do continue to produce the art works as for the passion and often the passion is what drives them. It would be ridiculous to think that any kind of financial incentives could power their creativity. However, not many of them are able to take up their passion on a full time. We should know that when their work is recognized, there will not be any dearth of money or fame.

In China, there is still a big gap between the poor and the rich, government should put more financial assistance toward the poor, which does not mean that providing assistance to artists is a waste of money. But now, we can give a true definition of artists at first, to extend this artist sense further, can we say a singer is an artist? In this way, quite a number of people would add up this population. Does the government has enough money to provide assistance to them?

All in all, it would be criminal to shun their creativity. It can be in the way of appreciation and opportunity to present their talent to the rest of the world. Our government should carry out some valid measures to deal with it.

（二）解决方法类议论文

模板 *1*

If you ________, what will you feel? Of course, you will feel ________ because ________. Besides this, ________.

For one thing, ________.

For another thing, ________.

No easy solution can be taken to cope with the problem of ________, but ________. Therefore, my viewpoint is that ________. For the ________ they should ________. For the ________, they should ________.

There is no doubt that ________.

分析：开门见山，指出问题的出现会给我们带来什么样的影响

从一方面说明原因

从另一方面说明

说明解决问题的困难性，表明我的观点

总结

模板 2

We must recognize that ________. Once ________, it is wise to ________. And yet ________.

To ________, we should first ________. Let's take ________ as an example. Besides, ________. It can result in ________.

To ________, we should also ________. Again let's take ________ as an example. So it is impossible to ________. However, no matter how difficult it is, we should ________. In fact, ________. Once ________, we should ________. Instead, we should ________.

分析： 强调我们要正确地重视问题

举例说明我们该如何做才能更好地达到目的

进一步解释说明

不管怎么样，我们都应该怎么做

模板 3

Most of us today recognize that ________ has been a greatly serious problem. Therefore, ________.

From above, we can find that the reasons why ________, are as follows, the primary reason, I think, ________. For example, ________. However, ________.

Second, ________. The third reason actually is the result of ________.

Therefore, ________. Moreover, ________. Let's make our good efforts, and ________.

分析： 强调问题的严重性，我们要提高重视

解释说明问题出现的原因，交代主要的原因并举例说明

提出第二、三个原因

总结，提出建议

模板 4

In contemporary society, ________ has become a serious problem in our country, ________. And it is not extremely astonishing for us to ________. Under such circumstances; these phenomena have already aroused public concern.

There are a quite number of factors, and the main reason is the ________.

To start with, ________.

Secondly, ________.

From my perspective, it is imperative for us to implement effective and efficient measures to ________. For one thing ________. For another thing, ________. All in all, ________.

分析： 开门见山，指出问题的出现和带来的影响

问题产生的主要原因

从两方面来解释其产生的原因

以个人的观点提出解决的办法

模板 5

As the rapid development of industry and economy all around world, ________ has become one of the most momentous problems every big city is confronted with.

To seek a better way out of the present straits, many proposals have been put forward to solve this problem. Some people suggest that ________. Some people insist that ________. Others propose that ________.

In my opinion, I am in favor of ________. For one thing, ________.

For another, ________. Besides, ________.

In conclusion, ________.

分析： 问题出现的原因和影响
交代人们提出的解决方法
我的看法及原因
总结

模板 6

People live in the world, ________ influence our life mostly, and we can see that ________. With the development of the technology, ________.

However, the changes of environment have caused quite a number of harmful effects. For example, ________. Besides, ________.

From now on, ________ is more pressing than ever before. ________.

Therefore, ________. Otherwise, ________.

分析： 问题的出现和带来的影响
转折，问题所带来的不好的影响，举例说明
加深说明问题的弊端
我们该如何解决

模板 7

It is well-known that ________. But nowadays ________ has become a serious problem in our country. What's more, it is frequently reported that ________.

It should be paid attention to that ________. On one hand, ________. On the other hand, ________. Therefore, it is high time that ________.

First of all, as for me, ________. This is because the ________. Secondly, ________. Thirdly, ________. Only in this way can we ________.

分析： 总述不良的现象和这个现象出现的背景，提出并说明出现这一现象的具体表现

说明这一现象的危害和产生的原因，从两方面阐述危害和原因，并说明解决问题的必要性

指出三种解决的办法并进一步说明解决问题的根本途径

模板 8

One of the most challenging problem of today's society is the ________. It is not only ________ but also ________. I would like to ________.

First, ________. The advantage of this model is that ________.

Second, ________. In this model, ________.

Another way of solving the problem is ________.

One further solution is ________.

In fact, I must admit that ________.

分析： 揭示问题的出现并说明原因

阐述自己的观点

说明解决的方法
总结

模 板 9

Nowadays, ________ is changing rapidly. As a result, ________. Scientists believe that this is the result of ________

In my opinion, there are three ways to solve this problem. Firstly, ________. As well, ________.

Secondly, ________.

Finally, ________. For example, ________.

In summary, it is clear that ________.

分析： 问题出现的原因和科学家的认可
介绍我认为可行的解决办法一
解决办法二
总结

经典范例

Directions: *In the recent years, the housing problem has been a hot topic in most big cities. Many people argued that the price of the building is too high, some people argue that argument should adopt some courses of action. Give the reasons and make some suggestions.*

As the rapid development of industry and economy all around world, housing problem has become one of the most momentous problems every big city is confronted with. More people are swarming into some big cities. Accommodations have become ever difficult, which is causing inconvenience to people's work and life.

To seek a better way out of the present straits, many proposals have been put forward to solve this problem. Some people suggest that more high buildings should be constructed. Some people insist that the underground be developed. Others propose that satellite cities be built. Still others argue that cities should be expanded to move people to the suburbs.

In my opinion, I am in favor of building the satellite cities in the suburbs. For one thing, these satellite cities are not far away from big cities. For most people, the traffic is fairly convenient for them to go to the downtown as they wish and do their works, shopping and other leisure things.

For another, the fresh air and adequate space there will be great attractions for people who are living in crowded cities. If many people move to the satellite cities, the housing problem in big cities will cease to exist. Besides, compared with other suggestions, building satellite cities could not only save a lot of energies, but also provide good environment for people to live.

In conclusion, to some degree, government should control the price of housing and commodities so as to more and more people could afford to buy buildings. In addition, government should also carry out a rounded measure to draw up this plan and assimilate local people's advice as much as possible.

（三）评论类议论文

模板 *1*

In our society, ________ is still regarded as the most important ________, but ________. For example, ________.

In my opinion, I think ________. Such as ________. As a result, ________.

(________ not only ________ but ________.) Besides, ________. Generally speaking, ________.

In a word, ________. Therefore, ________

分析： 评述问题的出现带来的不同看法
我对此的评论
进一步举例说明问题
总结

模板 2

With the development of ________, ________ are involved in it. But when it comes to ________, there are different opinions on it.

Some people maintain that ________.

Meanwhile, as is well-known, a person's energy is limited. So, ________.

But other people don't think like that because ________. For instance, ________. In a word, ________.

分析： 开门见山，提出问题的出现产生的影响
说明一些人赞成这个观点的原因
进一步举例说明
另外一些人不赞成这个观点的原因和看法

模板 3

It is well-known/true that ________, such as ________. Therefore, we should ________.

Many remarkable reasons contribute to this argument. First of all, ________. For example, ________.

What's more, ________. Besides, ________.

What we should do is ________.

分析： 描述现象的产生，举例说明问题所在，表明我们的态度

强调很多事实验证了这个评论，举例说明
进一步阐述
我们要做的是什么

模板 4

________ is becoming more and more popular and it has got into people's life. More and more ________ are now working on ________.

In the most cities, ________ has been taking shape. Some people ________. Others ________.

Now, ________ will be developing dramatically. It's estimated that ________. Therefore, ________.

分析： 提出问题的出现，已经进入了人们的生活
进一步举例阐述问题，交代一部分人的看法
说明另一部分人的看法
对问题的评价和估计

模板 5

There is no complete argument among people of ________. Some people consider that ________. However, others think that ________.

Some people may say that ________. They hold the opinion because ________. However, others believe that ________. They argue that ________.

Personally, I am in favor of the former opinion. Firstly, ________. Secondly, ________. Most important of all, ________.

Taking the above-mentioned factors into consideration, I may reasonably conclude that ________.

分析： 开门见山，提出观点的产生，指出人们的看法

说明其中一些人的看法，指出他们坚持这个看法的原因，还有另外一些人的看法及原因

我个人的看法和原因

全文总结，提出自己的建议

模板 6

More and more people begin to choose ________, so ________ are very popular in ________. Therefore, ________.

Compared with ________, ________ have many advantages. Firstly, ________. Secondly, ________. What's more, ________. In addition, ________.

However, ________ also create some problems. Therefore, we have a long way to go to solve the problem.

分析： 开门见山，说明越来越多的人开始选择和关注

举例进行对比，说明优点，进一步讲述优点

转折，说明它同样给生活带来困扰，还要进一步解决

模板 7

It is well-known that ________, but nowadays ________.

It should be paid attention to ________. On one hand, ________.

On the other hand, ________. Therefore, ________.

First of all, ________. In addition, ________. Moreover, ________. Only in this way can we solve the problems faced by ________.

分析： 总述评论焦点的产生

强调我们要注意的方面，从一方面表明原因

从另一方面阐述说明

总结做出结论

模板 8

There is no denying that ________ have/has become controversial, not only ________ but also ________. Some say that ________ while others ________. I am in favor of discussing this issue ________.

For the people who ________. Moreover, ________. In addition, ________.

For the people who ________. Besides, ________.

From the above discussion, we can easily conclude that ________.

分析： 提出问题，表明人们的看法，提出自己的想法

一些人的看法

另一些人的看法

总结

模板 9

________ as well call it recently, has made the headlines frequently.

Many people applaud it and argue that ________. They think ________.

However, ________. For example that ________. And it is possible that ________.

Since ________. The decision ________ makes about ________ will undoubtedly have tremendous influence on society.

分析： 引出这一现象的产生

提出一些人的看法和观点

转折，表明这一现象所带来的不好影响，举例说明

阐述这一现象的出现给社会带来了很大的影响

模 板 10

________ has long been a custom for ________. However, these years the Chinese people have different opinions about ________.

Some people think that ________ is good thing. In their eyes, ________. Also, it adds ________.

Others, on the other hand, ________. The main reasons are that ________, but also may cause troubles. For example, ________.

In my opinion, ________. We must try our best to find new beneficial ways to ________.

分析： 引出问题的出现已经成为一种风俗，并且说明不同的人有不同的看法

一些人认为这个观点是对的，说明原因

而其他的人从三个方面进行阐述相反的观点，举例说明原因

我的看法并提出一定要尽我们的努力来找到有利的途径去解决

模 板 11

Now it is common to ________. There is no consensus of opinions among people as to the view of it.

People who ________ have their reasons. Some people are in favor of the idea. First, they think that ________. Second, ________. That is to say, ________. Third, ________.

But others may not agree. Those who ________. For one thing, ________. For another, ________.

Judging from the above, ________. Certainly, there is little doubt that further attention will be paid to this issue.

分析： 大家对于问题给出不同的看法

举例说明支持这种看法的原因

举例说明不支持这种看法的原因

提出结论

模板 12

The issue of ________ is a complex and sensitive one. One's attitude towards it would largely depend on ________. As different people have different understanding on the ________, there are bound to be perennial discussions of the pros and cons of growing.

An argument often ________. For example, ________.

On the other hand, ________. For example, ________. Moreover, ________.

Personally, I think ________. Without suggesting that ________. I believe that ________.

分析： 提出问题，不同的人有不同的看法

具体说明一个评论，分析其原因

从另外一个方面说明

我对评论的看法

模 板 13

________ have more and more difficulty in ________. Nevertheless, many others insist that ________.

Proponents of the former view believe that ________.

Opponents of this view argue that ________.

Personally, I trend to argue with ________. Firstly, ________. Secondly, ________. In a word, ________.

分析: 说明问题的出现给人们带来的影响

一些支持者的观点

一些反对者的观点

我从两方面的评述

模 板 14

It is ture that ________ can create serious social and environment problems, the question is to discuss ________.

Some people would agree that ________.

The problem with this approach, however, is that it is very difficult to know ________. For example, ________.

Another problem is that ________.

________ is/are essential for ________. The best approach is ________.

分析: 肯定问题给社会和环境带来的影响，提出主题

一些人的评论

问题在人们提出的方法中所带来的困难，举例说明

指出另一个问题的关键

总结，最好的方法是什么

模板 15

It is well-known that ________, just like ________. In my opinion, ________.

________, for example, ________. We cannot imagine that ________.

However, /On the other hand, ________. On the contrary, ________.

To conclusion, ________.

分析: 提出问题和我的观点

强调问题，举例说明

从另一角度说明

总结评论

模板 16

There has long been a discussion about ________. Different people hold different ideas on this practice. Personally, I think there are some valid reasons in this argument.

On the one hand, ________. Besides, ________.

On the other hand, ________.

Let us reflect in another way, ________. In addition, ________.

The root of the problem ________. For these reasons ________.

分析: 提出问题，交代大家对评论的看法及我的态度

从一方面进行阐述

从另一方面阐述

从另外的角度说明

指出问题的根本，我们该如何对待

经典范例

Directions: *Some people believe that personal happiness is directly related to economic success. Others believes there are other factors. Discuss both views and give your opinion.* (2006. 12. 16)

Almost everyone wants to be happy in their whole life, and happiness is must be in our life. However, what is happiness? Different people have different ideas to define it. Some people think happiness from seeking fame and profit. Other people are happy when they have a harmonious family. They treat people wholeheartedly and find happiness from it.

In my opinion, according to philosophy, everything is in process of development including happiness. People could feel happiness at any time when they have found their love or met their idols and so on. However, what most people pursue is the eternal happiness.

Then how to obtain happiness? Firstly, I think true happiness can be got from a lot of aspects in our life, such as when a woman became pregnant; the most happiness thing for her is to safely have her baby.

Secondly, happiness is rooted in optimistic attitude. In our growing process especially when we became adults, we should face a lot of problems, which may lead to setbacks. If these defeatist sentiments seize us, happiness will be far away from us. The only way is right attitude and sparing no effort to overcome it then you can find happiness.

Last but not least, happiness comes from our good mood. We should to learn how to make ourselves keeping a right attitude in point, and the life will makes us happy and cheerful.

All in all, happiness is very important to our life. Everyday the more spirit and passion we have, the more happiness we would like to enjoy.

(四) 提问类议论文（同意与否）

模板 1

There are numbers of occasions on which we have to ________. Sometimes, others ask us for ________; sometimes, others ask us to do something that is ________. On all these occasions, we should ________.

However, in different reasons, most people have different ideas about ________. For some people, they think that ________.

For another people, they think that ________.

Personally, I don't believe that it is wise to hesitate when we should ________. On one hand, ________. On the other hand, ________. Therefore, I believe we should ________.

分析: 提出观点，并强调自己的观点，从两个方面进行阐述说明

指出不同的人有着不同的看法，说明一部分人的看法

另一部分人的看法

说明自己的观点并给人们提出建议

模板 2

________ has long been a custom for ________. However, these years the Chinese people have different opinions about ________.

Some people think that ________ is good thing. To their eyes, ________. Also, it adds ________.

Others, on the other hand, ________. The main reasons are that ________, but also may cause troubles. For example, ________.

In my opinion, ________. We must try our best to find new beneficial ways to ________.

分析： 引出问题的出现已经成为一种风俗，并且说明不同的人有不同的看法

一些人认为这个观点是对的，进一步论证他们的看法

而其他的人从三个方面阐述相反的观点，举例说明原因

我的看法并提出一定要尽我们的努力来找到有利的途径去解决

模板 3

How can one/Should one ________? The question puzzled almost everyone. In practice, (most) people ________

(Most) People consider ________, Besides, ________. Nor do they consider ________. In fact, they will choose ________.

A few people go to another extreme. ________. For them, ________. They won't ________.

For me, I won't follow either extreme. Instead, I will ________. That is to say, Thus, I will ________.

分析： 提出观点并表明它给人们造成的困扰

指出大部分人的看法和原因

少部分人的看法，他们与大部分人会选择不同看法的原因

指出自己的看法，不会选择任何一方，并说明原因

模板 4

________ as well call it recently, has made the headlines frequently. Many people applaud it and argue that ________.

They think ________.

However, ________. For example that ________. And is it possible that ________.

Since ________. The decision ________ makes about ________ will undoubtedly have tremendous influence on society.

分析： 引出这一现象的产生

提出一些看法和观点

转折，表明这一现象所带来的不好的影响，举例说明

阐述这一现象的出现给社会带来了很大的影响

模板 5

There is no denying that ________. However, we may find ________. Different reasons can be identified as contributing to this situation. The following reasons my view on ________

The most immediate reason for it being difficult for us is to ________. For example, ________.

An equally important reason that ________. It goes without saying that ________.

An additional reason that makes ________. For some people, ________. For the former, ________, while the later ________.

In view of the above reasoning, I am convinced that it ________.

分析： 说明问题的出现和影响，说明自己的看法

陈述最重要的一点原因

进一步说明

其他的原因

总结

模板 6

In major cities, problems with ________ are problems most people have to face every day. Some people hold that the principle reason for these problems lies with ________. They believe that ________.

Like anyone else, ________. In consequence, ________.

Moreover, the real cause of ________ is that ________.

In conclusion, ________.

分析： 提出问题的出现，带来的影响，人们的观点

进一步说明

强调真正的原因

总结

模板 7

It is commonly recognized that ________. Yet it is often the case that ________. I find it justifiable but do not share the opinion that ________.

It can be argued that ________. However, ________. As a result, ________.

Besides, ________.

Some people would argue that ________. In addition, ________.

In summary, ________.

分析： 提出并说明问题，表明自己的看法

其他的评论

一些人的评论

总结

模板 8

Presently there is a prevalent viewpoint that ________.

Unfortuately, /Fortunately I do find my agreement/agreement in this regard.

First of all, ________. However, ________.

Further, ________, Besides, ________.

The previous two arguments are based on ________.

分析: 指出自已对现在出现问题的观点

从第一点陈述

进一步说明

概括总结

模板 9

A prevailing phenomenon nowadays is that ________, which are becoming more and more assimilated. ________. As for me ________.

The drawback of ________. Some people ________. Others, ________.

On the contrary, ________ come up with many novel ideas countering the opinions mentioned above. ________. Besides, ________.

All in all, ________. It is my firm belief that ________.

分析: 提出问题的出现和影响，我的看法

指出不利的因素和人们的看法

相反指出一些原因

总结

模板 10

Many people believe that ________, and that ________. Personally, I do (not) agree with such a point of view.

In the first place, ________. In addition, ________.

In the second place, ________. Moreover, ________.

On the basis of ________.

分析： 大家对问题的看法，我个人的想法

从一方面说明

进一步说明

总结

模板 11

Some people argue that ________. Others dispute this. My personal opinion sides with the former/later.

First of all, ________. This is quite reasonable actually because ________. In other words, ________.

Also, ________. The reason lies in the fact that ________. Furthermore, ________.

In conclusion ________ should be held responsible for ________. However, ________. Hence, ________.

分析： 交代了争论的问题和我的观点

说明我同意/支持的原因

进一步说明

总结

模板 12

It is certainly true that ________. But I feel it is unfair to down play the role of other equally, ________.

In a sense, ________. For one thing, ________. For another, ________.

I am definitely (not) suggestion that it is ______. To some degree, ______.

________, which are as important as the ________ mentioned above. ________.

分析： 提出自己对问题的看法
从两方面来诠释问题
说明自己的建议
总结概括

模板 13

Some people question whether/what ________, refuting that ________. Instead, they believe that ________.

Even so, in some places, ________, inducating that ________. By way of forming my own opinion to the assigned statement, I will discuss the many virtues of ________.

It can be argued that ________. First and foremost, ________.

In addition, reports have shown that ________. For example, ________. Finally, it is important to ________.

As I mentioned above, ________. Thus, ________.

分析： 提出问题以及人们对它的看法
举例说明原因并指出自己对它的一些优点陈述
具体说明自己的观点
通过报道来进一步说明
总结

模板 14

Taking ________ is widely recognized as ________. Nevertheless, I am thoroughly in support of above statement and will endeavor to exemplify my opinion on this matter throughout the following discussion.

With ________ becoming increasingly more competitive, there are many ________. Indeed, there has been ________.

I think that people's understanding of ________ has changed dramatically in ________. Last but not least, ________.

The important thing to ________ is that ________.

分析: 说明问题的出现已经广为人知，并交代自己的观点

具体说明原因

提出人们对其的看法和观点

指出重要性

模 板 15

The booming ________ has brought about ________. In my opinion, however, ________.

Of course, ________ has/have a lot of barriers. The first barriers for ________ are ________. Therefore, ________.

Another obstacle is ________. As a result, ________.

All things discussed above, ________.

分析: 交代问题产生的原因和自己的态度

问题带来的一些障碍，并进一步说明

具体介绍另一个问题

得出结论

模 板 16

It is commonly recognized that ________, is based on ________. We can not deny the fact that ________. Still, I don't think ________.

Statistics in ________ indicate that ________. It is widely accepted that ________. Admittedly ________.

Besides, it is even more debatable to ________. We should not neglect that ________. It is only reasonable and necessary that ________.

In conclusion, the idea that ________.

分析： 介绍问题出现的原因，强调是我们不能忽视的事实，表明我的态度

通过调查显示表明具体原因

对问题产生质疑，说明原因，并确定我们应该怎么做

总结

模板 17

Recently, there has been a discussion about ________. Most people hold that ________. In my opinion, I do feel that ________.

One reason is ________.

Besides, ________, such as ________.

Another reason is that ________, therefore, ________.

In sum, ________.

分析： 提出人们争论的焦点，大部分人的看法，我的态度

说明我有这样看法的原因之一

另一个原因

做出总结

模板 18

Nowadays, ________ are thorny issues in every major city all around the world. To combat such problems, ________.

First, ________. The government should work out a strategy, such as ________. In addition, ________.

Second, it is reported that ________. Therefore, ________.

To conclude, it is (not) the best way to ________ because ________.

分析： 交代问题的出现给人们带来的不好影响
从其中一点说明，政府应该采取什么样的策略
从另外一点说明，通过调查来说明问题
总结，强调有（没有）一种方式来解决，并简要说明理由

模板 19

Nowadays, ________. Therefore, ________. In my point of view, ________.

Firstly, ________.

Secondly, ________. In addition, ________.

There is no doubt that ________. Therefore, I emphasize that ________.

分析： 交代问题，表明我的态度
从第一点分析
从第二点说明
强调结论，并表明毋庸质疑的态度

模板 20

In the modern society, ________ has spread rapidly into our lives. ________. Therefore, there arises a fierce debate concerning the proposal that ________.

As far as I am concerned, firstly, ________. Secondly, ________. Thirdly, ________. In a word, ________.

Despite the benefits ________, many people have strongly opposed idea of it, saying that ________. First of all, ________. Secondly, ________. Consequently, ________.

To be frank, ________. In my mind, ________

分析： 提出问题并说明问题产生的原因
根据个人观点分析说明原因
一些持反对意见的人的看法
做出评论

经典范例 *1*

Directions: *Housing shortage in big cities can cause severe consequence. Some people think that only the government can solve this problem. To what extend do you agree or disagree?* (2006. 5. 13)

Nowadays people in urban areas are confronted with severe housing problems such as shortages of spaces and the inferior quality of buildings. These problems will no doubt lead to moral or economical crimes and increase the insecurity of citizens. As to whether only the government should take on the responsibilities to cope with the problems, there arises a controversial discussion that draws the public's great concern.

Advocates hold the opinion that it is only the government's obligation to deal with housing problems. For one thing, only the government has the ability to call for experts in relative fields to get together and present their ideas on this issue. The government can also provide enough funds and equipments when necessary during the process of problem solving. For another, one of the government's unique functions is legislation. The government can standardize behaviors in constructing and purchasing so that the serious situation will be controlled to some extent. Besides, it is generally believed that policies of housing made out by government are authorized and convincing. Therefore they are much easier to be implemented.

Opponents, however, argue that the government shouldn't be the only one to work out housing problems. To start with, government officers have to deal with problems in all aspects of the development of local area every day. If the government is required to concentrate on solving housing problems, its workload will be increased and many other problems cannot be solved effectively. Additionally, other professional institutions like real estate companies may have more professional and practical views on this issue. It is essential to make full use of their functions. Moreover, solving problems together will increase the awareness of social responsibility and sense of belonging among the citizens. Unity is an extremely important factor for the development of the whole society.

Personally, I side with the latter because a satisfied situation of housing is closely related to the benefits of individuals. Thus our joint effort is urgently needed.

（2006 年 5 月雅思 7 分作文—外语教育网）

经典范例 2

Directions: *Increasing the price of petrol is the best way to solve traffic and pollution. What extend do you agree or disagree?*（2006. 6. 17）

Nowadays, bad traffic and increasing pollution are thorny issues in every major city all around the world. To combat such problems, government encourages companies to mark up gas price in an effort to decrease car use. Although it may temporarily alleviate the problem, it is doubtfully the optimal solution.

First, the number of cars in a country directly depends on the proportion of the population. As a result, raises in gas price could invoke hard feelings among this segment of people but would not drastically change their behavior in using cars. The government should work out a strategy, such as we should have more and more construction of better roads and effective use of available transport facilities.

In addition, we can use the cheaper and cleaner energy resources although we have a very long way to reach such technological area.

Second, it is reported that waste gas from cars is not the leading cause of air pollution, and the real culprit is the rapidly growing manufacturing industry. Therefore, reduction of the number of cars would not return us a blue sky and fresh air. We could better handle this problem if we could increase control over industrial waste discharge and adopt more environmental friendly materials and production equipment.

To conclude, it is not the best way to control traffic and pollution by increasing gas price because such action will influence consumers and economy without achieving what it is aimed for. Such measures I discussed above like construction of better transport facilities could be more effective solution to be considered.

经典范例 3

Directions: *It is right that college graduates earn higher salaries than the less well-educated in the community. But they should also pay the full cost of their study. Do you agree or disagree with this statement?*

It is commonly recognized that salary or income, in most cases, is based on contributions made by people to companies or organizations in which they are employed. We cannot deny the fact that higher level of education, indeed, do associate with better income. Still, I don't think college graduates should be fully responsible for their expenses.

Statistics in the labor market indicate that people with professional training tend to find jobs easier than college graduates do, and some employers prefer to hire and pay more to highly skilled and specially trained people rather than fresh college graduates. It is widely accepted that people's income is determined more by talent and hard work. Admittedly in some knowledge extensive field such as research, teaching, and practice of law the labor force primarily consists of highly educated professionals. But such people make up only a fraction of the labor market and are thus unrepresentative of the whole employment in general.

Besides, it is even more debatable to throw all the responsibility of financing college education to college students. We should not neglect that all the parents contributes to the education system in various ways. It is only reasonable and necessary that the country gives some forms of financially assistance to students to ease the burden of rising education costs, which would act the funded college education's attraction, and boost the motivation of children from millions of families to engage in higher level of study.

In conclusion, the idea that students should also pay the full cost of their study is wrong, what we should do is to take responsibility in financing college education so that the goal of higher education will be better met.

经典范例 4

Directions: *Many scientists believe that now we can study the behavior of a three-year-old child to see whether they will grow up to be criminals. To what extent do you think the human nature produces crime? And how can we prevent the children from growing up to be criminals?* (2005.8.13)

A lot of crimes are still happened everyday all around world. Crimes undermine human society. A crime is varied and complex. In my mind, we could not say that violation of law is just human nature.

We are not sure what causes people to commit a crime. It is reported that the reason in cases in which a thief steals money in order to make a living or on an impulse to do such silly things. Many of them, when caught, reveal that they come from poor families or have something wrong with their psychological health. People used to believe that parents could teach their children the harms of wrongdoing by showing them the consequences of such action and the obligation of complying with social norms. But we also see that many high-level officials take bribes or abuse power for their own benefits, and such people with high income and good education clearly know what they are doing and the possible consequences. Crimes would not have happened if tendency to commit crimes could be stopped when people were young.

Moreover, if the crime is human nature, people live in mountainous district without much education would commit crimes at a higher rate than people with more knowlege in cities. By contrast, people in remote places are more honest and kind, and the crime rate is significantly lower than that in city. From such evidence, we could not conclude that the above assertion is true.

To sum up, the conclusion is we should not support that it is human nature to commit crime and that people's tendency to break the law could be stopped. The researches of what causes crime and how to prevent it are continuing to explore for us, we need to bear in mind that it is far more complex than we normally think.

经典范例 5

Directions: *Nowadays, teenagers cause a lot of social problems due to lack of discipline. Some people think that parents should spend more time staying with their children. Do you agree or disagree?* (2004. 7. 10)

Nowadays, most parents have one child, and have their jobs to pursue high quality living conditions, not only for themselves, but more important for the family. Therefore, the parents try their best to offer their children comfortable circumstances, but they seldom have enough time to stay with their children. In my point of view, no matter how busy they are, they should make the best use of their time to stay with their children.

Firstly, communication is one of the most important ways to improve the relationship among all the people especially between children and adults. Children could feel parents' affection through the genial conversation and sharing their pleasure with them. What parents should do is help them to prepare their birthday parties, applaud for them when they are competing in the sports meeting or get good marks.

Secondly, children need the right direction from their parents. There are some wrong behaviors in our society such as dishonesty, corruption and so on. Children have weak resistance in defending this harmful influence. In this case, parents' instructions seem to be very important to children's growth. At this time, parents should talk with them about what they should do and should not do. In addition, if parents often spend time in staying with their children, adults' good behaviors will greatly influence their children.

There is no doubt that there are some disadvantages in spending too much time on children. For example, some parents give them little freedom to develop their interests and even more to form dependence on their parents. Therefore, I emphasize that parents should educate and instruct their children appropriately in their spare time apart from their busy works.

（五）利弊议论文

模板 *1*

It is a new thing that ________. Many people applaud/welcome this new development while others have expressed their concern about this.

Those who take sides against this new trend believe that ________ because ________.

One common argument, however, for ________ is that ________.

Of the two views discussed above, I'm in favor of the ________. My reason is that ________. If ________ he or she has to ________.

分析： 不同的人对问题的出现持有不同的看法

反对的人的看法

支持的人的看法

综上所述，说明我的看法和原因

模板 2

Everyone wants to be ________. ________ has become much more popular. The benefits of ________ are numerous; it is especially beneficial for ________.

People today are ________. To avoid ________, we should ________.

However, ________.

In short, if done correctly, ________. It will become an important part of our life.

分析： 直接提出主题，表明其带来的好处和产生的影响

阐述更多的人的倾向，为了避免不好的情况出现提出方法来解决

转折，提出恰当的和不恰当的方法所带来的影响

总结并建议用好的方法

模板 3

In the recent years there has been an increasing wave of ________. That is partly because ________.

There are many advantages/disadvantages of ________. First, ________. Furthermore, ________.

On the other hand, ________.

In a word, in my opinion, ________. Furthermore, ________.

分析： 表明最近出现这一现象的趋势和原因
指明这一现象的优点/缺点
从另一个角度继续阐述
总结（简单说明问题带来的优点/缺点）

模板 4

________ is developing rapidly in China. With the reform and opening-up policy being carried out, thousands upon thousands of ________ are crowding into ________.

________ brings a lot of benefits. From one thing, ________. As we know, ________. Besides, ________.

From another thing, ________. It is clear that ________.

However, everything has two sides. ________ gives rise to a number of problems. For instance, ________. Besides, ________.

In my mind, ________.

分析： 说明现象出现的原因
从两方面具体说明现象带来的好处
现象同样给我们带来不利的影响
我的总结

模板 5

Everyone has their own ________, some people like to ________, while other people are fond of ________. As far as I am concerned, both of them have their own advantages and disadvantages.

On the one hand, ________.

Besides, ________.

On the other hand, ________.

In conclusion, ________.

分析: 提出问题，交代人们的不同看法以及我对它的态度

从一方面说明优点（缺点）

进一步阐述

从另一方面说明缺点（优点）

总结

模板 6

With the development of our modern society, ________. Of course, ________. There are two viewpoints about ________. Some people think that ________. In my opinion, both of them are partially reasonable.

Someone believes that ________.

Others insist that there are undoubtedly some disadvantages (advantages) in ________. First, ________. Second, ________.

Judging these two viewpoints above-mentioned, I think ________. Under such conditions, ________.

分析: 直接提出主题，大家的观点，我的看法

具体说明一些人的观点

从两方面说明问题的优缺点

综上评述，做出结论

经典范例 1

Directions: *Nowadays many students have the opportunity to study for part or all of their courses in foreign countries. While studying abroad brings many benefits to individual students, it also has a number of disadvantages. Write an essay analyzing the positive and negative effects of studying abroad.*

In recent years there has been an increasing wave of quite a number of students choosing to study abroad. This is partly because more and more people want to learn the western cultural and party due to the variety of grants and scholarships which are available for overseas students. Although foreign study is not something which every student would choose, it is an attractive option for many people.

There are many disadvantages of studying overseas. First, they cannot adapt to the customs in one foreign country, especially in some western countries, because that is quite different from our native tradition. Furthermore, by looking abroad students may find a wider range of courses than those offered in their country's universities, and therefore one which fits more closely to their particular requirements.

On the other hand, studying abroad has a number of drawbacks, which may be divided into personal and professional. Firstly, it will spend a long period for students to leave their family and friends. Besides, studying abroad is almost always more expensive than studying at one's local university. At last, students often have to study in a foreign language, which may limit their performance and mean they do not attain their true level.

In a word, in my opinion, the disadvantages of studying abroad are usually temporary in nature. Students who study abroad for one year or even longer will become proficient in the language in a short time and they also can learn how to be independent. It is the best way for them to become more experienced and have their eyes on something in future.

经典范例 2

Directions: *Do the negative effects of some international media such as TV and magazine for example overweigh the positive effects? Write an eassy to state the positive and negative effections of them.* (2006. 11. 25)

International media such as TV and magazine has been one main medium that has connected all the people around world. More and more people tend to concern it. Like many other things, media is double-edged.

As primary channels of information, TV and magazine are convenient in our daily life. Interestingly, sometimes the same piece of information varies considerably in its influences on audiences of different ages. For example, many advertisements are shown on TV, for the buyers, the advertisement is useful and attractive because they might be spending time searching for such products in shopping and making decisions, which make them save time by making use of such advertisement. Yet, for the young children, they could have misleading understanding on these advertisements; they don't know the use of the products. Worse yet, these are classic bad influences of media for young people's overspending and inappropriate behaviors for their future.

However, we find it very difficult to weigh between advantages and disadvantages of media, because they are often closely incorporated. For instance, we often see violent scenes in movies, which are detrimental effect on young people. In contrast, a lot of movies also release their anger, anxiety, and pressure. Moreover, these movies show us bad and evil as well as punishments for wrongdoings, and we cannot imagine that if we live in a world whose media is completely clean in such sense.

In conclusion, media should not be seen simply as bad or good because we need to use information properly. At the same time, we should be very careful with regard to the content of information and take measures to keep viewers from possible harmful influences of media.

第二节 应用文模板（G 类 Task 1）

一 分解句型模板

✻ 常用开头模板

1. I am excessively sorry to tell you that…

   我非常抱歉地告诉你……

2. Now, I am writing you this letter of apology to show my deep regret.

   我现在写这封信是为了表达我最深的愧疚。

3. Please accept my sincere apology with gratitude. I hope you will…

   请接受我真诚的歉意，我希望你能……

4. I am applying for the position of…

   我要申请……

5. I look upon it was a wonderful opportunity.

   我把它看作一个非常好的机会。

6. It was certainly grand of…I appreciate it all the more.

   这是个很好的……我更加欣赏它。

7. I am sorry to occupy your precious time, but I really want to talk about…

   我很抱歉占用您的宝贵时间，但是我真的很想说……

8. I am a ... student and wishes to study at your prestigious university.
我是……（学生）我很希望能在贵校学习。
9. I have learned with delight that you...I would like to extend to you my utmost congratulations on... You must be proud of... And I feel happy for you.
我很高兴得到你……的消息，我想表达我最诚挚的祝贺……你一定对……感到骄傲，我也为你感到高兴。
10. I am writing to complain about ... And ... Your agency promised that...
我写这封信是为了投诉……，……你们机构已经答应了……
11. Welcome to...to begin with，...it is my pleasure to...
欢迎……首先……是我的荣幸。
12. I am writing to express my dissatisfaction with...
我写这封信是为了表达对……的不满。
13. There are some problems with the...that I wish to bring to attention. For one thing，there is... For another，...
……有些问题，我希望您能注意一下。一方面……有……，另一方面……
14. I can hardly bear/tolerate/put up with it any more.
我不能再忍受了。
15. I regret to inform you that I am unable to do...
我很抱歉告诉你我不能……
16. I have read your advertisement in...*Daily* for a position of a...
我在……上看见你们刊登的招聘……职位的广告。
17. I wish to apply for the position of...which you advertised in yesterday's...*Daily*.
我想申请你们昨天在……上刊登的……职位。
18. I am very interested in exploring the possibility of obtaining a

position as a…with your company.
我对在贵公司获取……的职位很感兴趣。

19. I read with interest your advertisement which appeared in… and would like to take up the challenge as a…with your firm.
我对……上你们的广告很感兴趣，我愿意接受在你们公司……的挑战。

20. Your university is a well staffed and well-equipped institute with a long history and a fine tradition of scholarship, enjoying a worldwide fame I will certainly feel greatly honored if I am fortunate enough to be admitted into it.
贵校是一所师资强大、设备齐全、历史悠久且奖学金完善、享誉很高的大学，我很荣幸若能有幸加入贵校。

21. Would you please let me know the procedures for admission at your earliest convenience?
您能让我尽早得知入学的一些程序吗?

22. I am writing to inquire about the possibility of being accepted as a graduate student in your university upon my graduation.
我写信想咨询一下贵校能否接受一个毕业生。

23. I wish to pursue my Master's degree in your university.
我想在贵校获得硕士学位。

24. Thank you for your email of…
感谢你……的邮件。

25. I'm writing to invite you to my…
我写信想邀请你参加我的……

26. I write with my suggestions about the improvement of service of your hotel as requested in the letter you sent me last Monday.
受你们上周一信中的请求，我致信你们酒店对服务上的改进提出了我的建议。

27. I am writing to inquire if you have already made a decision.
我想咨询一下你是否已经做了决定。

28. I am writing to express my views on the limited varieties of the food at your…where I have dined in the past week.

我写信来是想说一下，上个星期我用餐的时候，我发现你们……的样式很少。

✻ 常用结尾模板

1. We would be grateful if this matter would have your immediate attention.

   如这个问题能够引起您更快的重视，我会很高兴的。

2. With your…I am sure that you will be a success in whatever you undertake.

   因为你……我肯定你在什么方面都会取得成功的。

3. My best wishes for your future success.

   对你未来的成功表示我由衷的祝福。

4. I look forward to your reply and to attending your esteemed university soon.

   期待您的回复，并期望很快加入贵校。

5. I wish all of you the very best and thank you all for listening. Thank you!

   给予你们最好的祝福，感谢你们的倾听，谢谢。

6. I'll write to you, …my thanks to…for your many kindness to me.

   我给你写信是关于……我很感谢你的热情。

7. I hope that you will consider me for your position. May I have a personal interview at your convenience? I look forward to hearing from you.

   我希望您会考虑我担任您的职位，在您方便的时候能给我进行一个单独的面试吗？我期待着您的答复。

8. I want to suggest that… I shall be obliged if you will kindly write and tell me… We may meet again and I hope to see you

again.

我想建议……。如果您愿意写信告诉我，我会很高兴的，我希望再次和您见面。

9. I hope that the authorities concerned will consider my suggestions and improve the situation as best as they can.

我希望政府部门能够考虑一下我们的建议，尽可能地把条件变好。

10. I sincerely hope that… will review its management system, with the view to providing better service to the public.

我真诚地希望……能够审查一下管理系统，以便为公众提供更好的服务。

11. We trust that you will now consider this matter seriously and make an effort to prevent the recurrence of this kind.

我们相信你会认真地考虑这件事并且能为阻止此类事件再次发生做出努力。

12. We will appreciate your willingness to make up for the loss.

我们将十分感激您能主动补偿我们的损失。

13. I am awfully/terribly sorry for what I have done.

我非常抱歉我的所作所为。

14. I feel very guilty for what I have done to you.

我很内疚对你做的事。

15. I am afraid what I have done has caused many inconveniences to you.

恐怕我做的事情给你带来了很多不便。

16. Please accept my most cordial and humblest apologies for… once more.

请再次接受我诚恳的歉意……

17. I will try my utmost not to make such a stupid mistake again.

我会尽我所能不再犯这样愚蠢的错误。

18. I am so sorry to have put you to so much trouble.

我很抱歉给你带来这么多的麻烦。

19. After completing my four-year course at…university in 2003, I was employed by ABC company as a…
我于 2003 年结束了在……大学四年的学习后，进入 ABC 公司担任……一职。

20. I believe I have the appropriate qualifications and experience for this post, and therefore, here I am enclosing my curriculum vitae.
我相信我有合适的条件和经验能够胜任这个职位，这个是我的履历表。

21. Upon graduation, I first worked as … The following job was…, and currently I am working for…
毕业后，我第一份工作是……接下来是……现在我在为……工作。

22. I am available for an interview every afternoon. Please contact me at…
我每天下午都方便面试，请联系我……

23. I hope that after reviewing my enclosed resume you will kindly give me an interview so that I can elaborate on my studies and working experience.
我希望您看过我的简历后给我一个面试的机会。以便我能详细地和您说说我的学习和工作经验。

24. I hope you would consider my application favorably and grant me an interview.
我希望您会考虑我的申请并给我一次面试的机会。

25. With the kind of experience I have accumulated, I would expect a salary of not less than…
我积累了足够的同类经验，我希望我的工资不低于……

26. I would greatly appreciate it if you would forward the necessary materials and relevant information at your earliest

convenience.

如果你能够尽早把一些有用的资料和相关信息发给我，我会不胜感激。

27. If you need any additional information, please do not hesitate to contact me.

如果你需要任何其他的信息，请及时联系我。

28. Thank you from the bottom of my heart for your kind help.

衷心感谢您的帮助。

29. I wish there were a better word than "thanks" to express my appreciation for your generous help.

"谢谢"二字已不能表达我对你帮助的感激。

二 背诵经典全文模板

(一) 道歉信

模 板

Dear ________,

I am writing you this letter to express my apology to you for ________. Please accept my sincere apology with gratitude. I hope you will understand me.

The reason is that ________. Therefore, ________.

So I am terribly sorry that ________. I really regret that I ________. In addition, ________.

I do hope you can forgive me.

Signature

分析: 表达自己的歉意，诚恳希望对方能够接受道歉

说明做错事的经过

表明承认错误的态度及补救的方法

（二）求职信

模 板

Dear ________,

I am applying for the position of ________ advertised in ________. I cannot think of a better job I'd like than a programmer for a company like yours. I look upon it was a wonderful opportunity.

My major is ________ that definitely meet your qualifications. My complete resume is attached.

I was graduated from ________ and I am a hardworking person, ________. I am a capable of programming in ________. I believe my training and experience will enable me to perform better than other candidates who lack working experience. You will find me to be reliable and efficiency.

I hope to meet with you to discuss the possibility of working at your ________. You can reach me at my home phone, ________, any day ________.

I hope that you will consider me for your position, and look forward to meeting you in the near future.

Signature

分析： 直接申请广告中的职位，肯定招聘公司，表明自己要抓住这个机会

介绍自己的教育背景、工作能力以及一些工作经验，并肯定自己，强调自己符合要求，说明已经随信附详细简历

恳请对方给予自己面谈的机会

告知对方联系方式，盼望答复

（三）感谢信

模 板

Dear ________,

I am writing to thank you for ________.

________. It was sweet and thoughtful of you to think of it.

It was great ________ and my thanks to ________ for your much kindness to me.

Thanks again.

Signature

分析： 直接表达为什么事情表示感谢

再次叙述事情的经过和自己的心情

再次表达自己的感激之情和真挚的祝福

（四）建议信

模 板 *1*

Dear ________,

I am sorry to occupy your precious time, but I really want to talk about ________.

In my opinion, ________. On one hand, ________. On the other hand, ________. It is true that ________. If we don't ________.

I hope you can help to put an end to this situation and restore our confidence in ________. And I am sure ________.

I am looking forward to your reply.

Best regards.

Signature

分析： 先提出对占用时间表示歉意，但还是想表明自己的想法

说明自己写信的原因

希望能够早点解决，并肯定会有好的解决办法

期待回复

模板 2

Dear ________,

I am delighted to learn that ________. I propose that you apply for ________. To begin with, ________. What's more, ________.

In order to study ________, you have to meet the following requirements. In the first place, ________. In the second place, ________. Last but not the least important, ________.

As far as I am concerned, first, ________. In addition, ________. Only through these measures can you hope to ________.

Signature

分析： 表达自己很高兴听到这样的消息并提出自己的建议

提出自己对如何更好地得到这个机会的建议方法

总结自己的经验，表达自己的愿望

(五) 申请信

模板 1

Dear Sir/Madame,

I am ________. In the previous one and a half years I have been ________.

However, since I registered here, the expenses have become a burden for my average family. You know, ________. Therefore, I must ________. In addition, ________, I guarantee that ________.

I would be greatly obliged if my application is granted. Thanks.

Signature

分析: 介绍自己的情况

申请的原因和金额，和自己的保证

表示感谢

模板 2

Dear ________,

I write to submit my application for the ________.

I graduated in ________ with ________ and spent ________ of my career working for the ________.

I have punished ________ and also ________. Besides ________. I also take ________.

I believe that the advanced and technology and particularly the valuable experience I would gain from purching my ________ would put me in ________. I would be more grateful if my application could be taken into consideration, and I am looking forward to your reply.

Signature

分析: 简要说明申请的目的

具体说明请求的原因

希望对方能够尽快答复，并表示感谢

（六）祝贺信

模板

Dear ________,

I was so happy to hear of the good news of you that

________. I would like to extend to you my utmost congratulations on ________. And I feel happy for you.

________ is quite exciting news! You are ________, I know this is surely owing to ________.

I am sure that you will be a success in whatever you undertake with your ________, and I hope that ________. My best wishes for your success.

Signature

分析： 得到值得祝贺的消息，说明祝贺事由，表达自己的祝贺，描述对方的心情和自己的心情

对祝贺人所取得的成绩，进一步阐述祝贺的事由，对对方的赞美

表达对对方的信心和祝福，咨询对方的情况并表达自己的愿望和美好的祝愿

（七）投诉信

模板

Dear Sir or Madam,

I am writing to complain about ________. ________ and ________. Your agency promised that ________.

________, however, ________. I find it dishonest and unacceptable that ________.

The receipts which are enclosed ________ and in addition, we claim a refund of ________, because ________.

We would be grateful if this matter would have your immediate attention.

Signature

分析： 抱怨的内容和原因

抱怨内容的几个方面，表明自己看法

向收信人提出索赔
表达本人的愿望

（八）咨询信

模 板

Dear ________,

I am writing the letter for ________. So I want to consult you about some information.

I am concerned with ________, and I am eager to know ________. Would you please let me know ________? In addition, ________. How can I ________?

Thank you for your time on my enquiries. I am looking forward to hearing from you soon.

Signature

分析： 介绍自己写这封信要咨询的原因
说明想获得自己感兴趣的信息
表达自己渴望得到信息的心情和对对方的感谢

（九）邀请信

模 板

Dear ________,

On behalf of ________, I am greatly honored to have the pleasure to invite you to ________. You are requested to ________.

The place is ________ and the date is ________. As we all know, you succeed in ________ and we would like you to ________.

I hope to hear from you at your earliest convenience.

Signature

分析： 诚挚地邀请对方参加活动

活动的相关细节并说明与对方相关的细节

期待对方的答复或者征求对方对邀请的意见

（十）推荐信

模 板

Dear ________,

I am writing to you to recommend ________.

Now he is looking for ________ in ________. I have known ________ for ________ and I can truthfully say I have never met a much younger person than he/she is. Whenever ________, he/she always ________. Moreover ______.

Therefore, I don't hesitate to recommend her/him as an ideal candidate for the post.

Signature

分析： 表明自己想要推荐某人

介绍自己与被推荐人之间的关系，对被推荐人印象及他或她的特长、表现等

希望对方能够考虑自己的推荐

（十一）请求信

模 板

Dear ________,

I am writing to formally request to ________.

The reason for ________ is that ________. what is more,

________.

(I would also like to request ________, because ________, and ________. This decision was not changed lightly.)

Thank you for your attention to these requests. If you have any questions, please contact me at ________. I look forward to hearing from you soon.

Signature

分析： 说明求助的具体内容

讲述求助的原因

说明另一个请求和原因，并表明自己对它的重视

感谢对方为此事而付出的时间和帮助，并期待答复

(十二) 辞职信

模 板

Dear ________,

I am writing to inform you of my decision to resign from my current position.

The most important reason for my resignation can be listed as follows. Firstly, ________. Secondly, ________. In addition, ________. Finally, ________.

Thank you for everything you have done for me. I feel so terribly sorry for the inconvenience I have caused. I do hope that you will accept my resignation.

Best wishes to you!

Signature

分析： 说明自己要辞职的决心

具体说明自己辞职的原因

感谢原单位给予自己的帮助并表示自己的遗憾

表达自己的祝福

（十三）慰问信

模 板

Dear ________,

In today's newspaper, I read about the recent events in ________ and I am writing to extend my deepest condolences.

It broke my heart to ________. I couldn't believe my eyes when ________. I am really worried about ________. I am crossing my fingers for you now in hope that ________.

I can only imagine how difficult this time must be for you, and I want to extend to you my unwavering support. ________ is/are to donate money and necessary things to ________. I donated all my allowance that I have been saving for years.

I feel extremely sorry for this tragedy, and I will be looking forward to hearing from you.

Please pass my concern on to ________.

Signature

分析： 从报纸上获得的信息，表达自己的哀悼和伤心

进一步表达自己沉痛的心情并祝福受害者

提出捐助给予对方帮助

再次表达自己的心情，期待回复

送上祝福

（十四）公开信

模 板

Dear ________,

We found recently that ________. They are curious about ________. But they don't know that ________. Let's tell them

________.

Above all, ________. It is estimated that ________. (Financially, ________.) The cost thus becomes ________. What is more, ________. Finally, ________.

On the whole, ________.

Signature

分析： 指出问题的出现和出现的原因并提出警告

具体解释问题出现的原因和危害

总结，提出观点和建议

（十五）欢迎信

模板

Dear ________,

I'm delighted to learn that you are going to ________. And my parents will also be happy to see you again. I'm sure you will enjoy here completely.

I know you are fond of ________. I think it would be very pleasant and exciting to ________. ________. I believe you will ________.

Just phone me before you set off. There is no need for you to take anything. I'll prepare everything for you.

I am looking forward to seeing you soon.

Signature

分析： 对对方的到来表达自己的喜悦心情，并表明自己父母的心情和自己的是一样的，希望对方会开心

安排周到，提供几个让对方满意的建议，相信这样会给对方带来更多的惊喜和快乐

随时等待对方的到来，说明自己已经准备就绪

盼望到来

（十六）求学信

模 板

Dear ________,

I am a ________ student and wishes to study at your prestigious university.

First, what qualifications do I need for the study at your university? I already have a ________ degree from ________ university of ________.

Second, how much are the tuition fees?________. I would be interested to know if there are any scholarships. Third, what is the situation of accommodation?

I look forward to your reply and to attending your esteemed university soon.

Signature

分析： 介绍自己，表达自己申请到该校就读的愿望和自己的计划

开始介绍自己的情况和自己的一些学习能力

接着询问该校的一些情况，包括学费、奖学金和住宿问题

期待回复

（十七）寻找失物信

模 板

Dear ________,

I am writing this letter to request your assistance in finding my ________ which I have lost during the stay with your ________. Could you please check to see if my ________ has been found?

There are some very important things inside ________. You will find ________.

I would appreciate it if you could contact me as soon as possible. I would be greatful if you could ________.

Thank you for your help.

Signature

分析： 说明写这封信的原因，并希望对方能够帮忙解决
具体描述丢失的东西
表示自己的感激之情

经典范例 1

Directions: *You got a fever when you traveled to Shanghai in the first time, you must sign the contract in time, but you have to be sent to the hospital.*

Write a letter to the hospital. Thank all the staffs for their good care of you, which made you sign the contract successfully. You should write at least 150 *words.*

Dear Sir,

I am a business man from England, and my name is Thomas Smith. Last month I traveled to Shanghai for signing a contract with a Chinese industry company. Unfortunately I had a fever, because my temperature was nearly 40 degree centigrade, so I was asked to be in your hospital. During that time, I was afraid that the delay of signing the contact would lead to great losses to my company. However, after the doctors' careful treatment and nurses' patient care, I was recovered only in 2 days. So I completed the negotiation successfully and signed the contract on time finally.

I sincerely appreciate all the staffs in your hospital who helped me full-heatedly. I was deeply impressed by the kind doctors and nurses, the pleasant and comfortable environment, and considerate services. Although I have no relatives and friends in Shanghai, I felt at home in your hospital, which touched me deeply. I will always remember all those warmhearted persons and your hospital in my heart.

Best wishes to you all!

Faithfully yours,

David Smith

经典范例 2

Directions: *You bought a MP4 at the airport. On reaching home, you found a fault with it.*

Write a letter to the airport authority to explain the situation, and ask that the problem be put right. You should write at least 150 *words.*

Dear Sir/Madam,

I am writing to complain about a MP4 which I bought five days ago in the Duty free section of your airport. Your agency promised that if I found something was broken within one week, the MP4 could be returned to your company.

As my habit, I made a point of trying it out on the spot. It worked wonderful, however, when I got home and tried again, it seemed that the MP4 didn't work, and I find it dishonest and unacceptable.

I am sure that you will agree that this is a most unsatisfactory situation. Therefore, I request you to arrange to replace this MP4 with another new one, which must be in perfect working order. Failing that, I will have to insist on a refund in full price which I paid for it.

We would be grateful if this matter would have your immediate attention.

Yours sincerely,

Li Ming

经典范例 3

Directions: *You got a job as an English translator of business negotiation. But now you find that the work is not what you expected. You decided to quit.*

Write a letter to your boss, Mr. Wang, telling him your decision, stating your reasons, and making an aplogy.

Dear Mr. Wang,

I am writing to inform you of my decision to resign from my current position.

The most important reason for my resignation can be listed as follows. Firstly, I think the salary has proven to be much lower than you originally promised, and as you know, I have a large family to support. Secondly, my major is business English, I was always expecting to use my abilities to the full especially in business negotiation. However, my expectation has been proved wrong. In addition, all I have to do everyday is to copy some English files. Finally, I feel so disappointed and let out on the job itself as in the past three months I was never given any really important responsibility.

Thank you for everything you have done for me. I feel terribly sorry for the inconvenience I have caused. I do hope that you will accept my resignation.

Best wishes to you!

Yours sincerely,

Li Ming

经典范例 4

Directions: *You want to apply money from bank. Write a letter. Introduce yourself. Outline the reason and some plans for the* *application.*

Dear Sir/Madame,

I am a junior in Hebei University, majoring in English. In the previous one and a half years I have been a model student and the monitor of my class.

However, since I registered here, the expenses have become a burden for my average family. You know, my parents are both laid-off workers, and, what's worse, my father has suddenly fallen ill and is expecting a major operation. It will be beyond their ability to finance me through my remaining education. Therefore, I must relieve their financial pressure and that is my responsibility, now I am applying to your bank for a loan of 100, 000 yuan. If my application is approved, all the money will go to my tuition and fees for the coming academic years. In addition, I have made a detailed plan to arrange my school life, I guarantee that I will repay the loan within five years, please believe me.

I would be greatly obliged if my application is granted. Thanks.

Yours sincerely,

Li Ming

第三节 图表类模板（A 类 Task 1）

一 分解句型模板

✲ 常用开头模板

1. According to the chart, it is clear that…
   根据这个图表，可以很清晰地看出……
2. The chart shows the turnover of…
   这个图表说明了……的逆转。
3. Seen from the chart, it can be included that…

从图表中可以看出，它包括……

4. Among…, …account for…
在……中，……可以说明……
5. It has increased by…times as compared with that of…
与……相比上涨了……
6. There is an increase of…in total this year.
在全年有一个……的上涨。
7. It has been increased…
已经上涨了……
8. It would be expected to increase…times.
比预期上涨了……倍。
9. The table shows a…increase over that of last year.
这个表格显示出同去年相比上升了……
10. It was decreased…than that of the year…
与……年相比下降了……
11. The total number was lowered by…
总数目下降了……
12. It rose from…percent of the total this year.
全年上涨了……个百分点。
13. Compared with…, it fell from…to…percent.
与……相比，从……个百分点降到……个百分点。
14. The table shows the changes in the number of…over the period from…to…
该表格描述了在……年至……年间……数量的变化。
15. The bar/pie/flow chart/line curve illustrates that…
该柱状/扇形/流程图/曲线图展示了……
16. The graph provides some interesting data regarding…
该图为我们提供了有关……的有趣数据。
17. The diagram shows (that) …
该图向我们展示了……

18. The pie graph depicts (that) ….
该扇形图揭示了……
19. This is a cure graph which describes the trend of…
这个曲线图描述了……的趋势。
20. The figures/statistics show (that) …
数据(字)表明……
21. As is shown/demonstrated/exhibited in the diagram/graph/chart/table…
如图所示……
22. According to the chart/figures…
根据这些表(数字)……
23. As is shown in the table…
如表格所示……
24. As can be seen from the diagram, great changes have taken place in…
从图中可以看出,……发生了巨大变化。
25. From the table/chart/diagram/figure, we can see clearly that…or it is clear/apparent from the chart that…
从图表中我们可以很清楚(明显)地看到……
26. This is a graph which illustrates…
这个图表向我们展示了……
27. This table shows the changing proportion of…and…from…to…
该表格描述了……年到……年间……与……的比例关系。
28. The graph, presented in a pie chart, shows the general trend in…
该图以扇形图形式描述了……总的趋势。
29. This is a column chart showing…
这是个柱型图,描述了……
30. The graphs show a threefold increase in the number of…
该图表表明……的数目增长了三倍。

31. As can be seen from the line graph, …
由线状图我们可以看出……
32. The table shows the changes in the number of … over the period from…to…
该表格展示了从……到……期间数据的变化。
33. The table provides some data of…
该表格提供了有关……的数据。
34. As can be seen clearly from the table.
从表格中我们可以清楚地看出。
35. As can be seen from the table, great changes have taken place in…
从表格中可以看出，……发生了巨大变化。
36. The bar chart presents the general trend in…
该柱状图描述了……总的趋势。
37. As can be seen clearly from the bar chart, the fluctuation of… took place.
从该柱状图我们可以清楚地看出：……出现了波动。
38. This bar chart displays the numbers of…
该柱状图展示了……的数据。
39. The following diagraph shows the structure of…
该流程图展示了……的结构。
40. It always involves following steps.
它通常包含以下的几个步骤。
41. The whole procedure can be divided into…stages.
整个过程可以分为……阶段。

✲ 常用主体内容模板

1. To begin with, … Moreover, … In addition, … As a result, …
首先……，然而……，另外……，结果……
2. The negative effects of…are clear.

关于……的消极影响很明显。

3. In my opinion, I think that…
在我看来……
4. On one hand…on the other hand…
一方面……，另一方面……
5. be similar to…/be the same as…
与……相似
6. There are a lot similarities/differences between…and…
……与……之间有许多相似（不同）之处。
7. …has something in common with…
……与……在……方面有共同之处
8. The difference between a and b lies in…
a 与 b 之间的差别在于……
9. …（year）witnessed/saw a sharp rise in…
……年……急剧上升
10. As can be seen from the graph, the two curves show the flutuation of…
如图所示，两条曲线描述了……的波动情况。
11. Over the period from…to…the…remained level.
在……至……期间，……基本不变。
12. in the year between…and…
在……年到……年期间……
13. in the…years spanning from…through…
……年至……年里……
14. from then on/from this time onwards…
从那时起……
15. the number of…remained steady/stable from（month/year）to（month/year）…
……月（年）至……月（年）……的数量基本不变
16. The number sharply went up to…
数字急剧上升至……

17. The percentage of…stayed the same between…and…
……至……期间……的比例维持不变。
18. The figures peaked at…in（month/year）
……的数目在……月（年）达到顶点，为……
19. The percentage remained steady at…
比例维持在……
20. The percentage of…is sightly larger/smaller than that of…
……的比例比……的比例略高（低）。
21. There is not a great deal of difference between…and…
……与……的区别不大。
22. …decreased year by year while…increased steadily.
……逐年减少，而……稳步上升。
23. The situation reached a peak（ahigh pointat）of …%
……的情况（局势）到达顶（高）点，为……个百分点。
24. The figures/situation bottomed out in…
数字（情况）在……达到底部。
25. The figures reached the bottom/a low point/hit a trough
数字（情况）达到底部（低谷）。
26. …is…times as much/many as…
……是……的……倍
27. a increased by…
……增长了……
28. …increased to…
……增长到……
29. high/low/great/small/percentage
比例高（低、大、小）
30. There is an upward trend in the number of…
……数字呈上升趋势。
31. A considerable increase/decrease occurred from…to…
……到……发生急剧上升（下降）。
32. From…to…the rate of decrease slows down.

从……到……，下降速率减慢。

33. From this year on, there was a gradual declined reduction in the…, reaching a figure of…
从这年起，……逐渐下降至……

34. During the period from…to…
从……时期……到……时期。

35. …decline/rose（quickly）from…to…
……从……（猛烈地）上涨/下降到……

36. The number is…times as much as that of…
数目是……的……倍。

37. It has decreased…times, compared with…
与……相比，它已下降了……倍。

38. go up and down/wave/fluctuate/be unstable/be in flexible
起伏不定

39. The first point to note is the huge increase in the number of…
需要注意的第一点就是……数值的急剧增长。

40. The statistics show that…
这些数据表明……

41. form/comprise/make up/constitute/account for…percent
占百分之……

42. increase/raise/rise/go up/soar/ascend/mount/climb
增加

43. decrease/grow down/drop/fall/reduce/descend/shrink to/decline
减少

44. remain stable/stabilize/level off/remain unchanged
稳定

45. sharply/steeply/dramatically/drastically/suddenly
急剧地

46. considerably/significantly/noticeably/remarkably/rapidly
显著地

47. steadily/moderately/gradually/smoothly
稳步地，逐渐地
48. slightly/slowly/mildly/moderately
轻微地，缓慢地
49. The following diagram shows the structure of…
以下的图展示了……的结构。
50. It mainly consists of following steps.
它主要包括以下步骤。
51. The whole procedure can be divided into…stages.
整个的过程可以分为……步。
52. The number of…increased by…%
……的数字上升了百分之……
53. The number of…dropped by…%
……的数字下降了百分之……
54. The chart reflects several trends.
该图展示了几个趋势。
55. Over the period from…to…the…remained level.
在……至……期间，……基本不变。
56. The classification is based on…
是以……为基础分类的。
57. to be roughly classed under two heads
大体分为两类
58. to classify … into … categories（parts, kinds, types, characteristics, groups, classifications, aspects）/to fall into …classes/to be divided into…
分为……类（部分，种类，类型，特征，组，类别，方面）
59. to be graded according to…
根据……分级

✻ 常用结尾模板

1. As to me, I think that…
对于我而言，我想……

2. First of all, … Besides, … To conclude…
首先……。此外……。总之……
3. Such changes have a obvious impact on…
这些改变有个明显的后果在……
4. In a word, I should say…
总之，我想说……
5. However, there are a still a number…
然而，依然有很多……
6. We are so happy to see that the results becoming…
我们很欣慰地看到结果变得……
7. The data/statistics show (that) …
该数据（字）表明……
8. The data/statistics/figures lead us to the conclusion that…
这些数据资料令我们得出结论……
9. The tree diagram reveals how…
该树型图向我们揭示了如何……
10. Many reasons contribute to the phenomenon.
很多原因都能证明这个现象。
11. To sum up, the rise and fall of the percentage of smoking men and women in…. revealed, in general, a certain unpredicted trend.
总之，在……的男女吸烟的上升和下降百分率在总体来说，是个无法预计的趋势。
12. Overall, there is a massive growth in….
总体来说，在……上有个很大的增长。
13. General speaking, …witnessed a steady rise while…
总体来说，……见证了一个稳定的增长当……
14. The statistics lead us to the conclusion that…
由这些数据，我们可以做出如下结论……
15. It can be concluded from the bar chart that…
从该柱状图我们可以推导出……

16. From the analyses made above, the table offers a clear picture about…
从以上的分析可以看出，表格给我们提供了一个……清晰的图片。
17. When we study the chart, it is apparent that…
当我们研究这个图表时，我们很容易了解到……
18. To sum up, we can learn that….
总之，我们可以得到……
19. If we look at the number of…we can see a steady growth in numbers…
如果我们看看……的数字，就可以了解到在……数字上的稳定增长。
20. Most notably, according to the information in the graph, …
很明显，根据图表的信息……
21. In summery, it is obvious and noteworthy that…
总之，很明显也是很值得考虑的是……
22. since/now that…; I hope that…
既然……；我希望……
23. because of/on account of/owing to/thanks to + (doing) sth., I hope that…
由于……我希望……
24. …lead to/bring about/result in/account for…
……导致了/带来了……
25. (一个句子), therefore/thus/hence/as a result/consequently/(and) so…
……，因此……
26. …be caused by/result from/be the result of/be the effect of/be the consequence of…
……是……引起的/……是……的结果。
27. it is unimaginable that…
不能想象的是……

28. it is undeniable that...

不可否认的是……

29. it is interesting to discover that...

我们很有趣地发现到……

二　背诵经典全文模板

（一）表格类

模板 1

What is shown in the table above indicates/describes ________.

It can be seen from the table that the subjects for which the highest（average）scores were ________. However, ________. It is obvious that ________.

From the analyses made above, the table offers a clear picture about ________.

分析： 概括图表的时间段和研究的对象

指出最明显、最有意义的变化

针对变化概括总结

模板 2

This table represents the amount of ________.

According to the data, ________. On the other hand ________. Not surprisingly, ________.

When we study the chart, it is apparent that ________.

分析： 概括图表的总体情况——主要的对象和时间段

通过图表的信息，详细描写重点变化

总结

模板 3

The table reveals the information about ________ in ________.

The most obvious trend shown by the table is that ________. However, ________.

The other details shown on the table indicate that ________.

分析: 指出表格在整个时间段的变化

分别具体描述最明显的变化

说明图表的另一个变化趋势

注意: 在写图表类的作文时，首句一定要概括主题。中间部分要对极值点描述，最后作总结。

(二) 柱状类

模板 1

In this bar chats, we can see that ________.

According to the amount of ________, ________ are grouped into ________ categories. Those who ________, and the number in this group has been ________. The second group is those ________, their number ________.

To sum up, we can learn that ________.

分析: 介绍柱状图研究的时间和对象

把图分为几类来描述趋势

总结

模板 2

The bar chart above shows the number of ________. According to the information in the bar chart, ________ fall into/increase ________.

The number of cases recorded for ________ far surpassed the number of ________. Indeed, there was a steady ________ in ________.

If we look at the number of ________, we can see a ________ growth in numbers ________. Most notably, according to the information in the graph, ________.

分析: 交代柱状图主要说明的时间段和对象
根据柱状图描述各个阶段的数量的变化
通过其他数据说明变化

模 板 3

The bar chart illustrates the percentage of ________.

It is evident that ________ are the (lowest/highest) for ________.

By contrast, ________. Furthermore, it is important to notice ________.

In conclusion, it appears from the data that ________.

分析: 介绍了柱状图说明的时间和对象
通过比较描述主要的"最值"变化
从相反的角度描写变化
总结

模 板 4

The bar chart indicates many significant changes in ________.

A very noticeable trend was the steady increase in ________.

During the same period, there was a large ________.

It is clearly seen that ________.

分析: 介绍了柱状图说明的时间和对象

描述显著的变化趋势
在同一时间段的变化趋势
总结，描述主要的变化过程

（三）扇形类

模 板 1

As is shown in the pie chart above illustrates the different levels of ________. Compare the highest/ greatest/lowest/most/ smallest number/percent of ________. Apperently, ________.

In ________ (year), ________. However, ________. On the other hand, ________. (This is in stark contrast with the scenario in ________)

In summary, it is obvious and noteworthy that ________.

分析： 介绍扇形图的总体变化程度（要进行比较的对象）
具体说明变化趋势（通过最高和最低的比较进行描述）
总结（一句话概括总体情况）

模 板 2

It is clearly evident from the two pie charts above that ________.

In the first chart, ________. On the contrary, ________.

We can see from the second chart that ________.

In conclusion, the significant change in figures was ________.

分析： 介绍扇形图的总体情况
从第一个图形中得到的信息，相反，通过对比得到的信息

从第二个图形中了解到的主要信息
总结图形变化

模板 3

The pie chart reveals ________. The average spend can be divided into ________.

From the information described in the chart, it can be seen that ________.

The second greatest expense is ________.

分析： 交代了扇形图的对象，并且把图形分成几部分概括了总体情况
说明扇形图中最明显的变化
说明图形中第二大的变化，略带说明其他

（四）流程类

模板 1

The flow chart illustrates/indicates that ________.

From the chart, we can see that ________. ________, on the other hand, ________.

From the analyses made above, the flow chart illustrates ________.

分析： 说明流程图的主要内容
具体介绍流程图的内容
总结

模板 2

The diagram illustrates ________.

According to the figure, the first step of ________. Next,

________. Then, ________. Finally ________. The first stage is ________. The second stage is ________. And the last stage is ________.

Overall/In sum, the figure depicts the ________.

分析： 介绍说明流程图主要内容

详细说明主要过程

总结

注意： 流程图审题是关键的一步，第一部分把主题描述一下就可以了，而中间的部分也是按部就班的描述。

描述流程图过程的常用过渡性词语有：firstly、secondly、thirdly/finally、the first step is to、the next step is to、the last step is to、the first stage involves、in the next stage、in the following stage、in the last stage、first of all、to begin with、next、then、later、at the same time、simultaneously、subsequently、consequently、before this、during、after this、in the course of、in order to/in order not to、in order that、so as to/so as not to 等。

（五）曲线类

模板 1

The curve illustrates the number of cases of ________. / The curve graph compare ________ in ________. It is clear that ________.

In ________ (year), ________. On the contrary, ________.

In conclusion, the population of ________. But the ________ population of ________.

分析： 概括曲线图的总体情况和走势

具体描述变化（从两个曲线的变化进行对比描写）

总结

模板 2

As we can see from the graph, the two curves show the fluctuation of ________.

Over the period from ________ to ________. There was a slight increase ________.

On the other hand, ________.

From the chart, it can be seen that ________.

分析： 概括曲线图的总体变化

具体说明第一条曲线的变化

描述另一条曲线的变化

总结

模板 3

The line chart describes the changes in ________.

According to the graph, over the period from ________ to ________ the trend was ________. There was a dramatic ________. From ________, there was a more ________ in popularity of ________.

In contrast, there was a ________ trend in the number of ________.

分析： 描述了曲线的变化趋势

具体描述变化的阶段（首末两端的数据必须加入）

描述另一变化的曲线（直接做总结）

模板 4

The two graphs depict the same thing in two different ways. Both show the ________.

The first diagram simply records the amount of ________.

The trend is almost ________ from ________ to ________. The graph rises more ________ between ________.

The second gragh throws a new light on the situation. This line expresses ________. It reveals that with the exception of ________ was matched by a fall/increase. ________.

分析： 交代了曲线图的时间段和研究对象，并说明两个图的共同点

描述了第一个图的变化趋势（抓住关键点进行描述和数据的表现形式，不必全部描述）

描述了第二个图的变化趋势和两个图的内在联系

注意： 作总结的时候以一两句结尾，千万不要加自己的评论。

经典范例 *1*

Directions: *You should spend about 20 minutes on this task. Write your answer in a word processing program on your computer.*

The table below shows the results of a survey to find out what members of a city sports club think about the club's activities, facilities and opening hours.

Summarise the information by selecting and reporting the main features, and make any comparisons where relevant.

Write at least 150 words.

Club satisfaction survey table

Club activities	Female members	35%	35%	30%
	Male memebers	55%	40%	5%
Club facilities	Female members	64%	22%	14 %
	Male members	63%	*27%*	10%
Opening hours	Female members	72%	25%	3%
	Male`members	44%	19%	37%

The table compares the opinions of male and female club members about the services provided by a city sports club.

We can see from the responses that the male members are generally happy or satisfied with the range of activities at the club, with only 5% dissatisfied. In contrast, however, only about two-thirds of female members were positive about the activity range and almost a third were dissatisfied. The genders were more in agreement about the club facilities. Only 14% of women and 10% of men were unhappy with these, and the majority (64% and 63% respectively) was very positive. Finally, the female respondents were much happier with the club opening hours than their male counterparts. Almost three-quarters of them were very satisfied with these and only 3% were unhappy, whereas nearly 40% of the men expressed their dissatisfaction.

Overall, the table indicates that female members are most unhappy with the range of activities, while male members feel that opening hours are the least satisfactory aspect of the club.

经典范例 2

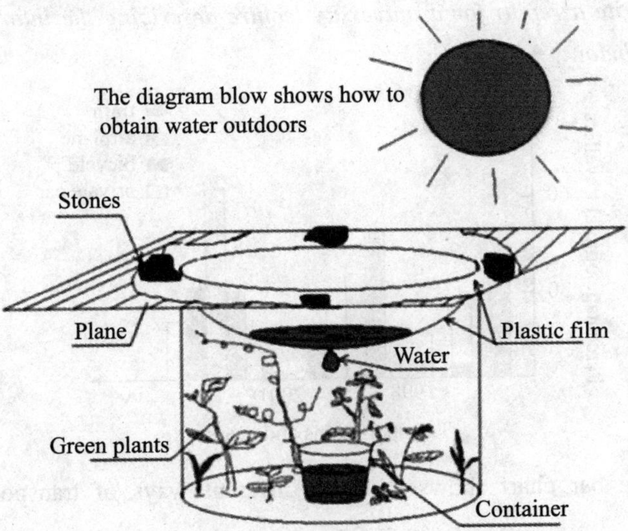

The diagram illustrates how water is collected in a container. The whole process is a cycle which can be divided into three main stages.

According to the figure, the first stage is to find a hole on the bottom with green plants. The second stage is removing the green plants on the middle of the bottom, and put a containcer there. And the last stage, use the plastic film to cover the hole, place four stones on each sides of the plastic film in oder to steady the position.

Water evaporates from these plants when the sun shines on the green plants into the hole, and the vapor cools down to form water drops on the plastic film. As a result, more and more water falls down into the container.

In sum, the whole process shows the effective use of water outdoors successfully through evaporation from the green plants.

经典范例 3

Directions: *The graph below shows the different models of transport used to travel in Beijing, in 1998, 2001 and 2004.*

Write a report for a university lecture describing the information shown below.

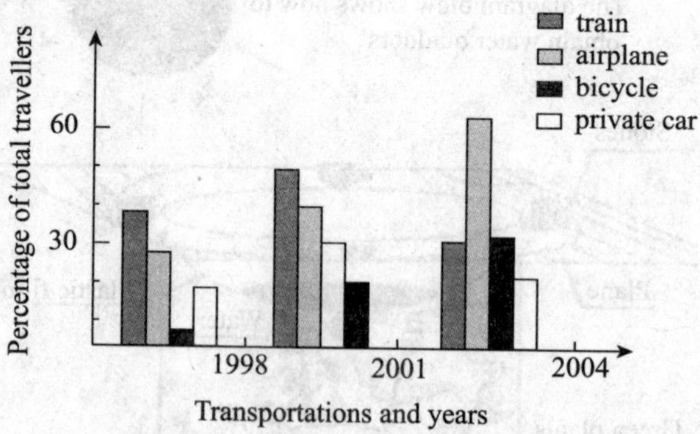

The bar chart shows that the different ways of transportation people in Beijing over 6 years, from 1998 to 2004.

As we can see from the bar chart, there are still a great number of people who choose train in the traveling, while those who traveled by private cars fluctuated.

In 1998, there were only 10% of people rode by bycicles. The highest percentage of people choosing train was accounted for 40%.

In 2001, there was a steady increase in each tranportantion. We can see a seeming surpurising ride in the number of people who by airplanes which stood at 40%. Those who chose bycicle and private cars are still have a lower percentage, increased by 10% respectively.

The year of 2004 witnessed a dramatic change. The number of people traveled by airplane continued to rise to 60%. The biggest drop went to those who by trains decreased from 50% to 30%. People who biked plunged from 20% to 30%, meanwhile, those who drove by private cars decreased 10%.

In conclusion, the transportation for people in Beijing to travel revealed some expected changes in the 6 years.

经典范例 4

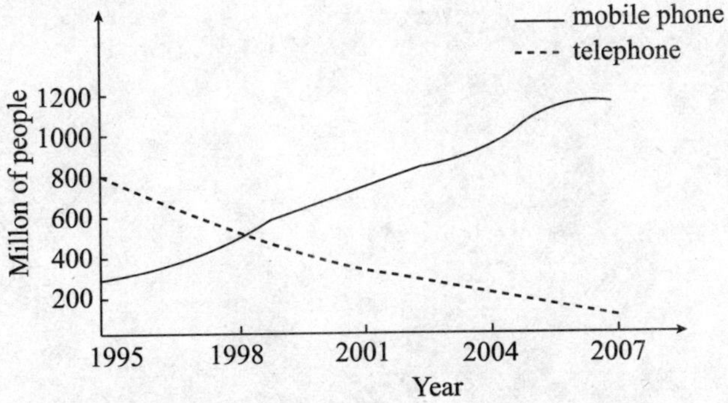

The changes in the popularity of telephone and mobile phone from 1995 to 2007

The line chart illustrates the trend of the popularity of telephone and mobile phone in America from 1995 to 2007.

As we can see in the line chart, there was a steady increasing in the popularity of mobile phone over the period from 1995 to 2007. On the contrary, there was a dramastic fall in the number of telephone from 1995, about 800 million people bought telephone. To 1998, and the figure was dropped to 400 million. From 1998 to 2001, the rates of decline slowed down. Moreover, there was a more gradual reduction in the popularity of the telephone, still reaching a figure about 100 million until 2007.

On the other hand, there was a rapid trend in the number of mobile phone in this period. In 1995 about 300 million and this figure rose steadily reaching 900 million. In 2004, to a peak of 1200 in 2007.

第三章　命题预测

预测一

Directions: *Nowadays, tourism has become the biggest industry all around the world. Unfortunately, international tourism creates tension rather than understanding between people from different cultures. To what extent do you agree or disagree?*

推荐模板

The booming ________ has brought about ________. In my opinion, however, ________.

Although it has become more popular than before, of course, ________ has/have a lot of barriers. The first barriers for ________ are ________. Therefore, ________.

Another obstacle is ________. As a result, ________.

All things discussed above, ________.

模板套用

The booming tourist trade has brought about mass population between different nations, which has become a popular thing all around world. In my opinion, however, this fast-growing industry has produced tension between people from different cultural background.

Although it has become more popular than before, of course, the tourist also has a lot of barriers. The first barriers for the tourists from all over the world are the problem of language and custom, as we know, which cause results in conflicts between tourists and local people. Therefore, the tour guide, normally interpreter too, becomes the only link of communication. But unfortunately, as indicated in any guide-training handbook, the responsibility of a tour guide is to arouse the tourists' interest and passion rather than present a lecture on cultural difference, which caused tourists cannot fully understand the cultures and also cut down the communication with local people.

Another obstacle is from the local government. In order to attract foreign investment and improve the local tourism industry, the local government, only hope to show these tourists the part of local living. As a result, these tourists, to some extent, have not their own free time to do they like, they allowed to see only what the organizers want them to see and no more. At this stage, the local government should ask tourists for advice before the traveling.

All things discussed above, the international tourism contributes nothing to increasing understanding. When we going to another country, be taught and understand the customs of that country is the most important thing to do.

预测二

Directions: *Do you think old buildings should be broken down, and give place for modern buildings. How important the old buildings are in our society?*

推荐模板

With the fast development of urbanization, ________. But many people argued that ________. In principle, however, I side with ________.

In the first point, to some degree, ________.

In the second point, ________.

In the third point, ________.

As mentioned above, I can draw a conclusion that it is necessary to ________.

模板套用

With the fast development of urbanization, many city planners advocate the demolition of old houses for the benefit of economic and social development. But many people argued that we can't ruin the traditional cultural heritage. In principle, however, I side with the former opinion.

In the first point, to some degree, the existence of old houses is an obstacle to modern urbanization. If our society have more modern breath, such as modern skyscrapers, the city will take on a new look. Take the Summer Palace in Beijing for example, as we all know, it is a time-honored symbol in China's traditional history, but now there are a large number of run-down of it till now, so the government demolish them instead of many new housing buildings.

In the second point, there is a potential danger to people living in old houses if the houses are old enough to collapse in the end, we can't see the value of culture from them, and the tourists surely will no longer to see these so-called "culture heritage" at the risk of their lives.

In the third point, replacing some old houses with buildings can help to solve housing problems. It is well-known that China is a densely-populated country and people in urban areas only have little housing space, therefore, which is a good way to solve the problem.

As mentioned above, I can draw a conclusion that it is necessary to replace old houses with modern buildings. At the same time, it is also necessary for us to restore a limited number of old houses or places of historical interest for the sake of conserving traditional culture and attracting tourists.

预测三

Directions: *In recent years, more and more advertisements have been flooding into our lives. Some advertisements exert negative effects. Therefore some people suggest that advertisements be banned. Do you agree or disagree with this? Give your reasons.*

推荐模板

In the modern society, ________ has spread rapidly into our lives. ________. Therefore, there arises a fierce debate concerning the proposal that ________.

As far as I am concerned, firstly, ________. Secondly, ________. Thirdly, ________. In a word, ________.

Despite the benefits ________, many people have strongly opposed idea of it, saying that ________. First of all, ________. Secondly, ________. Consequently, ________.

To be frank, ________. In my mind, ________.

模板套用

In the modern society, the advertising industry has spread rapidly into our lives. Every day we are surrounded by all kinds of advertisements, which have a profound influence on our daily lives.

Therefore, there arises a fierce debate concerning whether we should prevent from showing all kinds of advertisements on TV or not.

As far as I am concerned, firstly, some people are in favor of the idea that advertisement should not be prevented, instead, it should be further developed. In their opinions, advertisement is a good channel to exchange information especially in an era of information; everyone can benefit from not only the manufacturers but the customers. Secondly, the advertisement has become more and more attractive, people can know some of the newest products and the trend of consumption. Thirdly, as we all know, advertising, to some extent, is not only an industry but an art. Many advertisements are elaborate works of art full of originality, which render a wonderful visual feast to the viewers. In a word, the advertisement is a blessing for the modern people.

Despite the benefits advertisement has brought us, many people have strongly opposed idea of it, saying that they have been fed up with all kinds of rubbish advertisements. They hope to have a comprehensive ban on the advertisement based on the following reasons. First of all, a majority of advertisements are fictitious and misleading, interfering people's daily life and even leading to the injury and death of some customers. Secondly, advertisements bring many troubles to us. For instance, are you pleased with a wonderful film on TV when the advertisements are being interrupted frequently? Consequently, it will have an adverse impact on the younger generations.

To be frank, it is quite impossible for people to reach consensus on most controversial issues. In my mind, a total prohibition on advertisement is not a practical choice for us to tackle this problem. We could choose some health and useful advertisements, which don't last long time and the amount of advertisements should be limited.

预测四

Directions: *Many people believe that human activity is causing the earth's temperature to rise. They say that this global warming will have dreadful consequences for our environment, such as drought and flooding.*

What should government do to help prevent global warming? Give reasons for your suggestions.

推荐模板

Nowadays, ________ is changing rapidly. As a result, ________. Scientists believe that this is the result of ________.

In my opinion, there are three ways to solve this problem. Firstly, ________. As well, ________.

Secondly, ________.

Finally, ________. For example, ________.

In summary, it is clear that ________.

模板套用

Nowadays, the earth's temperature is changing rapidly. As a result, there have been a lot of climate changes such as heat waves, droughts and floods. Scientists believe that this is the result of human activity, which is polluting the Earth's atmosphere, and this is an immediate cause to lead to our environment become a disaster. If government does not act to help prevent global warming, we cannot imagine the worst result.

In my opinion, there are three ways to solve this problem. Firstly, more and more private cars appearing in the world especially in most big cities, and most pollution were caused from these cars.

So government should encourage people to ride bikes instead of driving cars, they should also support alternative sources of electricity from wind and water rather than from oil and coal. As well, some important organizations should sponsor conferences to discuss the effects of greenhouse gas emissions and solutions.

Secondly, they should make laws that limit the amount of greenhouse gases. The government could put some measures to most companies, and the companies should be rewarded for following these laws, or should also be punished for creating pollution.

Finally, everybody should put into this action. For example, everyone should save as much energy as possible by using more efficient light bulbs in our daily life, because that is our responsibility. Another way of saving energy is to increase public transport systems, government should spend money on public transport to make it as easy as possible for the public to save energy.

In summary, it is clear that there are a lot of things that government can do to prevent global warming and only by government and our efforts can make a better environment in the future.

预测五

Directions: *Unlike most countries, the police in the United Kingdom do not normally carry guns. Some people think it leaves the citizens unprotected, while others believe that this practice reduces the overall violence in society. Discuss both views and use your own experience and evidence.*

推荐模板

There has long been a discussion about ________. Different people hold different ideas on this practice. Personally, I think there are some valid reasons in this argument.

On the one hand, ________. Besides, ________.

On the other hand, ________.

Let us reflect in another way, ________. In addition, ________.

The root of the problem ________. For these reasons ________.

模板套用

There has long been a discussion about the policeman in the UK doesn't commonly carry guns when he is on duty. Different people hold different ideas on this practice. Personally, I think there are some valid reasons in this argument.

On the one hand, the policemen need guns in order to control crime. If police carry guns, the criminals could be deterred in time. Besides, it would make the criminals always have this mental in their minds, and sometimes they might quit before any danger things happened, so carry guns, to some extend, decrease some crimes.

On the other hand, for example, many countries with weak or ineffective gun laws, need a police force that is not only armed, but is armed better than the criminals. Otherwise, criminals are rampant in the country.

Let us reflect in another way, when police carry guns, there is possibility of a policeman's incidentally shooting an ordinary citizen. In addition, if the police carrying guns on duty, which might imply that the city people are living is so unsafe that they have to bring guns in order to protect themselves. That would certainly not good phenomenon for social stability in this country.

The root of the problem is embarrassingly corrupt government and seems to be a much more appealing option in the UK, because it maybe allows criminals to easily come into possession of guns. For these reasons nations around the world hope to reach the point where their police force can afford not to carry guns and still be effective someday.

预测六

Directions: *Sports and entertainment personalities have higher value than professional workers like doctors, nurse and teacher in some society. Discuss whether this development is good or bad to our society.*

推荐模板

It is well-known that ________, just like ________. In my opinion, ________.

________. For example, ________. We cannot imagine that ________.

However, /On the other hand, ________. On the contrary, ________.

To conclude, ________.

模板套用

It is well-known that many personalities have higher values in our society, just like sports and entertainment stars. In my opinion, though this phenomenon seems no fair to many people, some reasons could inllustrate it.

There is no profession in other businesses than being a star in the entertainment business that spends millions of dollars to promote a singer or movie actor. For example, movie stars or famous athletes entertain a nation or even the whole world, we can't imagine that their advertisement income of major concerts or sports events. Stars satisfy the needs of very large populations with greater efficiency than medical professionals or teachers, who usually work for one hospital or school. As a result, stars are able to create greater value for their employers.

However, the real value of many stars is more superficial. In the rapid development of the world, more and more new blood who have more potential than these famous stars. Furthermore, no matter how popular now, they would be forgotten as time goes by. On the contrary, professionals like doctors and teachers create the true value for our society, their experience and knowledge drive our society forward, and most of them are always set good examples for us especially for the young people.

Due to the powerful influences of show business, many young people are more interested in getting famous and rich overnight than working hard in other worthy professions. Such ideas and action would make young people throw away their ambition. To a certain degree, it is not good for their development in the future.

To conclude, the stars do not form the real value of a society. The true value of our world is created by people with real knowledge and skills like doctors and teachers. We should not encourage young people to waste time and money being stars instead of working hard to be someone more useful to their society.

预测七

Directions: *More and more parents would like to give pocket money to their children. Write an essay analyzing the positive and negative effects of pocket money.*

推荐模板

With the development of our modern society, ________. Of course, ________. There are two viewpoints about ________. Some people think that ________. In my opinion, both of them are partially reasonable.

Someone believes that ________.

Others insist that there are undoubtedly some disadvantages in ________. First, ________. Second, ________.

Judging these two viewpoints above-mentioned, I think ________. Under such conditions, ________.

模板套用

With the development of our modern society, people's living conditions become much more comfortable. So many parents give pocket money to their children when they don't have enough time to take care of their children. Of course, pocket money is useful to children, and children are considerable enough to make correct use of the money. There are two viewpoints about the pocket money. Some people think that giving children pocket money will make them become luxurious. Others hold the opposite idea. In my opinion, both of them are partially reasonable.

Someone believes that pocket money really has many advantages. Children can buy their daily necessities they like with this money. It also gives children a certain freedom to select what they want, make them aware rules of the equivalent exchange. Since time to parents is very precious, giving pocket money to children help them to be a person of independent means.

Others insist that there are undoubtedly some disadvantages in spending pocket money. First, young children do not know how to use pocket money appropriately and some parents cosset their children; they always give them a large amount of pocket money. Such conditions will make children think it is endless. Second, since adults do not supervise the procedure of shopping, children could probably buy something that is not suitable for their age.

Judging these two viewpoints above-mentioned, I think parents should give their children a limited amount of pocket money and they should instruct their children how to use the money moderately and what is suitable to them. Under such conditions, pocket money will do no harm to their children's growing.

预测八

Directions: *Some people think that young people should be taught to compete, but others think that young people should be taught to co-operate. Express some reasons of both views and give your own opinions.*

推荐模板

It is commonly recognized that ________ play a large role in advancement of our society. ________, however, ________.

It can be argued that ________. In addition, ________.

Besides, ________. For instance, ________. Therefore, ________.

From another point, we can see that ________.

In summary, in comparison, ________.

模板套用

It is commonly recognized that both competition and cooperation play a large role in advancement of our society. Competition forces people to challenge themselves in order to have good results. Cooperation, however, play an even more important role in development of individuals and the society as a whole, because it has become a principle in most places.

It can be argued that cooperation is a significant skill in the future life of young people. They will need work together or even live together; young people could gain more living experience or knowledge that they never met when they live alone, and they will feel happier than before. In addition, cooperation skills should be taught to face serious problems in the future.

Besides, cooperation is an important contributing factor to develop our society. While competition generally ends in a win-lose result. For instance, the competition would ultimately lead to the results that one becomes stronger and stronger, and other goes out of business. However, if the two companies cooperate with each other, they will become a larger enterprise; the more successful cooperation there is, the better the society develops. Therefore, cooperation should be taught to young people, because they will be the executive of cooperation.

From another point, we can see that most people are stressed by the competition, individuals has to survive, so they are compelled to try their best and make improvements.

In summary, in comparison, cooperation is more effective in helping individuals and societies to develop, because it benefits not only individuals, but also society as a whole.

预测九

Directions: *In the modern society, some people think that old people should not be forced by law to retire at the age of 55 − 60 if they wish* *to continue working. Do you agree with this point of view?*

推荐模板

Recently, there has been a discussion about ________. Most people hold that ________. In my opinion, I do feel that ________.

One reason is ________.

Besides, ________, such as ________.

Another reason is that ________. Therefore, ________.

In sum, ________.

模板套用

Recently, there has been a discussion about whether old people should be forced to retired from work at the age of fifty-five or sixty, regardless of their own wishes. Most people hold that old people should not go on working, for they have worked for over forty years, they should have more time to relax themselves. In my opinion, I do feel that the old people are physically and mentally, so they should not be forced to retire.

One reason is that people, whether old or young should have the right to decide their own way of life. Just as young people can choose their jobs and enjoy their leisure time as long as they can make ends meet, old people should also have their jobs if they like.

Besides, although many old people couldn't accept the fast speed of development of our modern society, there are still a lot of suitable jobs for them, such as some with more experience like consultants, instructors, and so on.

Another reason is that old people are not burdened with the financial pressure of making a living, they like to contribute themselves to do whatever they like. Therefore, some of them could utilize this time to keep them a good health and high spirits.

In sum, government should let old people do something that makes them happier, which not only to get a good environment for them, but also endure loneliness in their twilight years.

预测十

Directions: *Quite a number of people are interested in Online Shopping. Different people have different ideas of it. What is your opinion? Write an essay analyzing your idea.*

推荐模板

In the recent days, there is a growing popularity of ________. An increasing number of ________, and ________ has become one of the most important part in their daily life.

________ has attracted ________ was related to the following reasons. On the one hand ________.

On the other hand, ________. For example, ________.

However, ________.

In my opinion, ________, we can say that ________. If you want to ________, you had better ________. All in all, ________.

模板套用

In the recent days, there is a growing popularity of online shopping especially for the college students. An increasing number of people spent many hours surfing online with keen interest every day, and online shopping has become one of the most important part in their daily life.

Online shopping having attracted young people was related to the following reasons. On the one hand, with the global coverage of the

Internet, we can reach out and touch anyone at any place of the world. Many young people desire to buy their favorite things in the Internet because of its speed and convenience.

On the other hand, quite a number of newly things from all parts of world are shown online, which made more and more people want to possess these things. For example, when a person wants to buy a kind of camera, but he can't buy it in his city, by this time online shopping as his the first choice.

However, there are some disadvantages of online shopping, such as the pictures of goods shown on the computer screen are not what always they are, and it is not safe to pay by credit card online, because we don't know wheather the seller could sent the goods in time or not, after all, that is invisible transaction.

In my opinion, in this information age, we can say that if we don't have Internet, we cannot imagine our modern life. If you want to buy something online, you must careful when paying by credit card. In addition, you had better not buy very high-priced goods online. All in all, it can be not too careful to use online shops.

预测十一

Directions: *Nowadays, more and more people begin to choose doing more physical trainings in the gymnasium, because it really brings a lot of benefits. What is your opinion?*

推荐模板

More and more people pay more attention to ________, which not only ________, but also ________. Therefore, ________.

In the first place, as we all know, ________ is closely related to many things, such as ________. With the growing popularity of

________, more and more people begin to choose that for ________.

In the second place, ________.

In summary, as far as I am concerned, ________. Therefore, ________.

模板套用

More and more people pay more attention to their health in the recent years, which not only represents on the diet health, but also on their body health. Therefore, quite a number of people are doing exercises in the gym especially the young people. It is well-known that body-building makes us a high quality life in the modern society. People love and participate in body building; it spreads quickly in some developed cities. Personally, I am all agreeing with this trend.

In the first place, as we all know, body building is closely related to many things, such as politics. The spirit of the 29th Olympic Games are peace and friendship. At that time most people from all over the world will be together in Beijing. As the Olympic host, Beijing will present a kind of spirit that all the Chinese people are engaged into the Olympic Games. With the growing popularity of body building worldwide, more and more people begin to choose that for becoming stronger and stronger.

In the second place, in some big cities, most people have much more pressure in their working time, so when every weekend or vocation comes, they will spend a lot time to do practice, because everyone wants to keep a good and healthy body to confront more difficulties.

In summary, as far as I am concerned, doing more sports such as body building is a good method to keep our body shape and change one's state of mind. Therefore, body building has got a good impact on improving our living standard and our society's development.

预测十二

Directions: *Writes an essay, considering arguments for and against the following view: As reading is important for a good education, we should encourage our children to read whatever appeals to them.*

推荐模板

It is well-known that ________, just like ________.

However, everything has two sides; ________ bring some disadvantages, such as ________. We can imagine that ________.

On the other hand, ________. In a word, ________.

Consequently, ________.

模板套用

It is well-known that reading books can strongly shape your interests, mature your thoughts, widen your horizon and enrich your personality. Life is limited, but knowledge is boundless, just like the famous English philosopher Francis Bacon said, "Reading makes a full man." The more books we read, the more knowledge we get. Hence, we should encourage our children to read more books.

However, everything has two sides, books can also bring some disadvantages, such as some books contain evil thoughts and there might be much description about violence and superstition. We can imagine that if we are in the position of a parent. Would you allow your children to read whatever books that they like? I think the answer is "no". If children read bad books, the evil thoughts would possess their mind gradually, maybe they will be dispirited and perhaps commit a crime.

On the other hand, if the children read some good books, which teach and help them to have right directions to do something. All the parents hope their children have healthy and happy growing. Good books are children's real companions, and they are both instructive and inspiring. Children know past events from history books, study communication by language book, learn numbers through mathematics books. In a word, different kinds of good books can give them a large amount of ideas and knowledge.

Consequently, those who read good books can be inspired to grow healthily, while those who read bad ones will lead a wicked life and meet with miserable failure. Before we encourage the children to read books, we should choose the right books for them first.

预测十三

Directions: *Some people live in one community all their lives, while others move around almost as much as nomads. Both experiences have their advantages and disadvantages. What is your opinion?*

推荐模板

Everyone has their own ________, some people like to ________, while other people are fond of ________. As far as I am concerned, both of them have advantages and disadvantages.

On the one hand, ________.

Besides, ________.

On the other hand, ________.

In conclusion, ________.

模板套用

Everyone has their own living habits. Some people like to stay one place even by all their lives, while other people are fond of moving to new places, where bring new feeling and a good start. As far as I am concerned, both of them have advantages and disadvantages.

On the one hand, people who stay in one place for a long time could get good communication with other people, and they can develop lifelong friendships, furthermore, the greatest wealth is such friends may lend a hand if you have troubles, because they know each other's life habits, and they all willingly to do everything as much as they can.

Besides, spending a lifetime in one location can also lock a person into a limited way of life. It is difficult to change one's character. People with few experiences may develop a narrow outlook and find it hard to understand each other.

On the other hand, for these who moving frequently, although living in different places could have a variety of outlooks, it is usually stressful for them. A person may feel lost and don't have any safe feeling, for all the places were changed and there are no friends can help especially on special days, for example, if a person got one serious illness, he find that noboday could help him at that time, and the worst result is he died off.

In conclusion, for a person who moves to different places year after year, the disadvantages probably outweigh the advantages. But a few moves are probably worth the effort. By staying in one place for a long time, people can deepen their understanding and have enough time to make adjustment and form friendships.

预测十四

Directions: *The two pie charts below show the percentage of men and women in US who smoked during a 40 year period, between 1965 and 2005. Write a report for a university lecturer conveying the* *information in the two pie charts.*

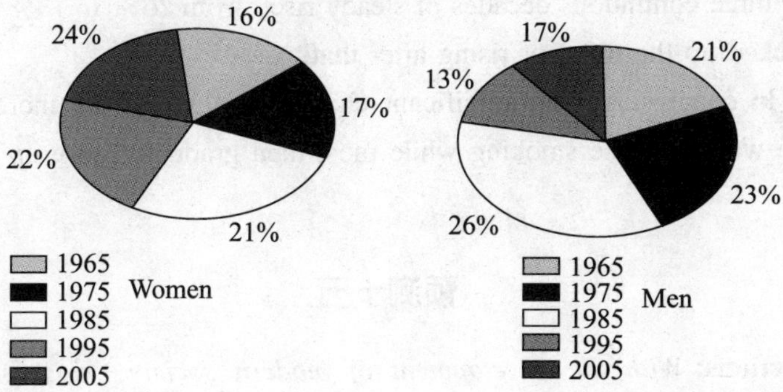

推荐模板

It is clearly evident from the two pie charts above that ________.

In the first chart, we can see that ________. On the contrary, ________.

We can see from the second chart that ________.

In conclusion, the significant change in figures was ________.

模板套用

It is clearly evident from the two pie charts above that the trend of both male and female smokers over a 40-year-long period of time, that is, from 1965 to 2005.

In the first chart, we can see that the percentage of female smokers was on a steady rise throughout the past forty years. On the contrary, the number of male smokers showed a trend of fluctuations.

In 1965, there were only 16% of female smoked cigarettes, and this ratio has got only 1% increase in 1975. However, there was a sharp increase in 1985. The year of 1995 witness another steady rise by only 1%, but another rapid climb in the next decade, from 22%

to 24%.

We can see from the second chart that there was a quick drop after three continuous decades of steady rise, from 26% to 13%. But it picked up the trend of rising after that.

In conclusion, the significant change in figures was more and more women chose smoking while most men gradually gave up it.

预测十五

Directions: *With the development of modern society, most people have become greed and selfishness, and we should return to the old traditions of family and community then we will have a better life. To what extent do you agree or disagree?*

推荐模板

The modern world is ________, but ________, such as ________, which ________.

On the one hand, ________. For example, ________.

On the other hand, ________.

As far as I am concerned, ________.

In sum, the most significant factor for ________. Therefore, ________.

模板套用

The modern world is full of vigor and energy, but many values are undergoing major changes, for example, more and more people want to be a successful person who has a lot of money, which causes modern people seem to be more self-absorbing and self-concerned.

On the one hand, modern people act selfishly to survive the

harsh competition of life. To survive, you have to fight with whatever means that come handy. Obviously greedy and selfishness go perfectly well with such ideas. For example, when a people work in a post, he does everything he can to get better pay and higher position. At this time, he is in any way advocating any selfish conduct.

On the other hand, in spite of common practice, it is hard to control that, because modern society is full of greed and selfishness, both of which are not newly words that we never met before. In ancient times, people also did greedy and selfish things though such behaviors were more condemned then. But we can not ignore the fact that people in the past lived a relatively more harmonious life, faced less newborn things and less competitive pressure among the people.

As far as I am concerned, selfishness is people's nature. If people should not be too selfish, we are happier to share with others and be generous to them. Caring for others can actually encourage the development of a mutually beneficial relationship.

In sum, the most significant factors for people be more self-centered than those in the past is strong outside pressure and desire. Therefore, we should encourage people to know the importance of being caring and generous to others and build a mutually beneficial relationship.

第四章　常用写作规范

第一节　写作格式规范

写作的主要要求有：

（1）在写每篇作文的时候，标题一定要放在文章的正上方，且不能用双引号，标题的后面也不能加逗号、下划线。另外标题的大写要准确。

（2）每个段落的第一行要向右边空4～5个字母的空格。

（3）标题和正文之间要空出一行。

（4）每个标点的后面要空出一个字母的空间，然后再写一个新的单词。

（5）整篇作文的上下都要留出两行空白，左右也要留出一个单词的空白。

（6）要注意字母大小写的区分：逗号之后要小写，句号后要大写，分号后面也要小写，文章最后要用句号做结束。

（7）当一个单词在这一行没有写完、想要移到下一行的时候，不能将一个音节分割开。例如："absent"就应该写成"ab-sent"。

（8）应用文中写信的要求很重要，下面就简单介绍一下写信时的要求：①信头。指发信人的单位名称、地址、发信日期。考试时候不要求写出。②称呼。信内地址下隔一两行写称呼，对不相识的男子，单数常用"Sir"、"Dear Sir"或"My Dear Sir"；复数常用"Dear Sirs"或"Gentlemen"。对女子，单数常用"Madam"、"Dear Madam"或"My Dear Madam"；复数常用"Mesdames"或"My Dear Mesdames"；对比较熟识的男子，普通称"Dear Mr. …"；女性通常称"Dear Mrs.（或Miss）…"。熟人和亲人常直呼其名。③正文。称呼下面隔两行开始写正文。每段第一个字母要缩进 3 ~5 个字母的空格。正文是信的主要部分，内容要简单明了，一般不用同汉语信一样的“你好（how are you?)”之类的词。④结束语。结束语是写信人对收信人的谦称，写在正文下面两三行处，从中间写起，第一个词的开头字母要大写，末尾用逗号。给不相识的人可用：“Yours truly”、“Yours faithfully”、“Yours Sincerely” 或“Sincerely yours”；给上级或长者可用：“Yours respectfully”、“Yours obediently” 或“Yours”；给亲属或挚友的信可用：“Yours affectionately”、“Lovingly Yours”。⑤署名。即写信人署名。一般情况下，把本人姓名签在结束语之下。

第二节　标点使用规范

一　句号

英语中的句号和汉语的不相同，英语中是一个实心的小圆点。句号主要用在陈述句、语气温和的祈使句以及带有直接引语句子的句尾来表示一个句子的结束。

如：More and more people begin to study English for Olympic Games in China.

注意：如果句子是以一个末尾本身有句号的缩略词结尾，那么句子结尾就不能再用句号，但是可以用其他标点。

如：Mr. Green grew up in Washington, D. C. , went to England at the age of twenty.

二　逗号

用来表示最短的停顿，主要用于：

1. 停顿并列的成分

如：I like shopping，cheating，and dancing in my spare time.（如果并列成分由 and 或者 or 连接，则不用逗号）。

2. 非限制性定语从句之前

如：I like her mother，who gets a good character.

3. 日期或者是地址中

如：The sports meeting will be held on Saturday，December 12，2006.

My boyfriend lives at 50 Sunshine Road，Tianjin，China.

4. 信件的开头和结束语

如：Dear Thomas、Truly yours、Sincerely yours

5. 句子插入成分前后

如：The director，however，didn't take his responsibilities to the patients.

6. 一个较长的修饰短语之后

如：In the middle of the coldest winter on record，the pipes froze.

7. 直接引用的句子之前

如：Mary said，"Let's go fishing."（如果句中含有间接引用就不需要逗号，如 Mary said we should go fishing.）

8. 反问句之前

如：He worked very hard，didn't he?

三 问号

问号用来表示问话的停顿或者加强语气。

问号要用在一个直接的问句中，而不用于间接的问句中。

如：How will you solve the problem?

注意：用在 I wonder how you will solve the problem? 就不对了，此句应该使用句点而不是问号。另外，在客气的问句用语中，也是用句点而不是问号，如 Will you please give me a call tomorrow.

四 冒号

用来引出一系列的并列句：

1. 用于对后面内容的介绍或解释

如：This is her plan: go shopping.

注意： 当冒号用于这样的目的时，它不能插入（系）动词和它的（表）宾语之间或者介词和它的宾语之间，如：Some different writing tools are: the pencil, the pen and etc.

2. 用于主标题和副标题之间

如：Web Directory: World and Non-U. S. Economic Data

3. 用于名单之前

如：We need seven people: three students, three engineers and a professor.

4. 用于数字时间的表示

如：16:45。

5. 在正式的信函中放在称呼的后面

如：Dear Vallen:

五 引号

包括双引号和单引号，用于标出别人的话或者文章中引用的词、词组或者句子：

1. 用于引用的书刊、文章、电影电视、歌曲的名称标题

如：This is a line from the poem "The West Wind".

2. 引用说话人或者作者的具体话语

如："OK," Thomas said to his mother, "if it can make you happy, I will do it forever."

3. 如果该词有特殊的意义，或者强调某个词时用引号

如：The wallet is always referred to as "she".

注意：（1）当“said”或者“reply”这样的附加语出现在被引用的句子后面的时候，该引用句应该以逗号结束。

如：“This is my answer,” he replied proudly.

（2）如果引用的句子是问句或者是感叹句，那么用问号或者感叹号结束引用语。

如：“Do you know he is a thief?” the police asked.

（3）如果这种附加语被放入一个完整的引用句之中，那么附加语前的引文部分以逗号结束，附加语本身也以逗号结尾。

如：“A woman's reaction in any crisis,” the major says, “is to scream.”

（4）引文结束时，句号和逗号总是被放入引号内，而分号或冒号总放在引号外，至于破折号、感叹号或问号。如果它们是引文本身的标点，就放在引号内，如果他们都是整个句子所需要的，就放在引号外面。

如：Several times the witness said, “I swear to the truth of my statement”; yet the jury remained unconvinced.

“Do you understand?” she asked.

Dose anyone understand what he meant when he wrote that “the earth belongs to the living generation”?

六 省略号

表示文中被省略的部分或者说话时的停顿和犹豫。

如：“Oh, no…” she said, then she was moved into tears.

七 括号

用来解释或者补充说明。它与破折号之间的区别是，破折号后面的部分是重点信息，而括号之内的信息却是次要信息。

如：A small mirror (a double-faced one) is useful to a camper for flashing signals or starting fires.

1. 表示列举时，括号表示顺序的含义

如：The word revolution means（1）a great, sudden social and political change by force,（2）a complete change in ways of thinking methods of working, and（3）circular movement round a fixed point.

2. 提供例子

如：He likes any kind of fruits (apple, orange, watermelon, or lemons), as long as it is fresh.

3. 对某一说法进行限定

如：First, it keeps you awake.（And I don't mean merely conscious; I mean wide awake.）Secondly, …

注意：如果括号内的句首不需要以大写字母开始，那么结尾也不用句号。相反，如上述例句中括号内首字母大写，则句末就要用句号以表示结束。

八 破折号

1. 用于解释的插入语之前

如：I know why my mother was so sadness — she was quarreled with my father.

2. 用于表示强调

如：It is really — really — disappointed.

3. 表示思想或语气的转折

如：The pardon from her boyfriend finally arrived — too late.

4. 表示语气的迟疑或者犹豫

如：He said to his mother hesitatingly, "I — I — I won't do it in the future.

5. 也可以用于表示列举，放在列举项之前

如：He has many good qualities — sincerity, honesty and

thoughtfulness — he had few friends.

九 分号

1. 分隔独立子句

分号用于分隔地位平等的独立子句，经常与连接副词 thus、however、therefore 一起使用（放在这些词语之前）。

如：I realize I need exercise; however, I'll lie down first to think about it.

2. 分隔相似内容

在句子中如果已经使用过逗点，为了避免歧义的产生，就用分号来分隔相似的内容。

如：The employees were Tom Hanks, the manager; Jim White, the engineer; and Dr. Jack Lee.

3. 连接两个主句

在 moreover、furthermore 和 however 之间用分号，以连接两个主句。另外，用分号和连接副词连接两个主句时，注意在连接副词之后用逗号。

如：I was still feel hungry; consequently, my mother give me an apple.

十 感叹号

用在表示强烈感情的句子、词组或词的后面。

如：How beautiful she is!

十一 撇号

1. 省略了字母

如：can't（cannot），I'm（I am）。

2. 表示复数形式

用在字母 s 之前，即 's 表示数字和字母的复数形式。如：

Tomorrow is Women's Day.

3. 表示所有格形式

用在字母 s 之前，即 's 也表示所有格的形式，在以 s 结尾的名词或复数名字之后，撇号表示所有格。如：my father's house。

第三节 数字使用规范

（1）如果一个数字的拼写不超过两个单词，则用拼写的形式，超过两个则用阿拉伯数字的形式。如：There are two days for me to take English examination. The classroom includes 150 desks for students to study.

（2）表示时间、日期、地址、百分比、页码等的时候。如：The 29th Olympic Games in Beijing will be held on August 8，2008. Everyday I get up at 6: 30 A. M. The Museum is located at East 23rd Street. Almost 90 percent of Chinese people have mobile phone. The name of the actress is appeared in Chapter 2 on page 23.

第四节 大写字母使用规范

（1）句子开头的第一个字母要大写。"I（我）"在句中任何位置都要大写。

（2）地名、国名和人名等专有名词第一个字母要大写。例如：Russia（俄罗斯）、Beijing（北京）、Jack（杰克）。

（3）一些亲属关系，用作称呼语时在人名前要大写。如：Uncle Tom。

（4）人名前的称呼或头衔第一个字母应大写。例如：Mr. Smith、Dr. Wang、Miss Mary。

（5）表示语种、民族的名词或形容词第一个字母要大写。例如：Russian［俄语、俄罗斯人（的）］、Chinese［汉语、中国人（的）］。

（6）直接引语中，句首的字母要大写。例如："Then," I said, "You have been making a mistake, and the letter is not in the apartment."

（7）星期、月份名称的第一个字母要大写，但季节第一个字母不要大写。例如：Sunday（星期天）、August（八月）、winter（冬天）、spring（春天）。

（8）一些大型节日名称的第一个实词的第一字母都要大写。如：Children's Day（儿童节）、National Day（国庆节）、Teachers' Day（教师节）。

（9）由普通名词构成的专有名词词组，除其中的冠词、较短的介词和连词外，每个词的第一字母都要大写。例如：the Great Wall（长城）、the United States（美国）。

（10）大型会议、文件、条约名称的每个实词（副词、介词、连词、助词、叹词和拟声词等虚词则不用大写）的第一个字母都要大写。书名、报刊的名称都要大写首字母，文章标题的每一个实词的第一个字母都要大写。如：China Daily（《中国日报》）、New York Times（《纽约时报》）。

（11）诗歌每一行第一个单词的第一个字母要大写。

（12）表示称呼语或职务的词首字母要大写。如：Mr. Green（格林先生）、Dr. Li（李博士）。

（13）大多数的缩略词要大写。如：CCTV（中国中央电视台）、ID（身份证）。

（14）"I"和"OK"在句中的任何位置都应大写。

（15）商品的商标名称要大写。如：Sony（索尼）。

（16）政府机构、院校名称要大写。如：Tsinghua University（清华大学）。

（17）表示重大历史事件的名词也要大写。如：The Renaissance（文艺复兴）。

第五节 缩写使用规范

写作中常用的缩写包括：

（1）人名的首字母缩写：Anan J. Christina。

（2）首字母的缩略词：IBM、BBC、CNN、AIDS、CPPCC、UNICEF。

（3）时间的缩略词：A. M. /a. m. 、BC、AD。

（4）当 Mr. 、Mrs. 、Jr. 、Dr. 和人名一起连用的时候：Mrs. Thomas、Kelly，Jr. 。

附　录

附录一　写作常用固定搭配表

一、动词固定搭配

1. break down 损坏；瓦解；（组织、计划等彻底毁坏）
2. break into 闯入，强行进入
3. break off 中止；中断
4. break out 逃出；突然发生，爆发
5. bring about 导致；引起
6. bring forward 提出；提议
7. bring to 使恢复知觉
8. bring up 教育，培养，使成长
9. call at 访问，拜访
10. call for 邀请；要求，需要
11. call off 放弃；取消
12. call on/upon 访问，拜访；号召，呼吁
13. carry on 继续下去，坚持下去；从事，经营
14. carry out 贯彻（理论等）；执行（计划等）；实现（目标等）
15. come across（偶然）发现；（偶然）碰见，偶遇
16. come on 开始；进展；上演；来吧；快点
17. come out 出版；结果是（to be）；出现；长出
18. come through 经历；脱险
19. come to 总计，达到；苏醒；复原
20. come up 发生；走近；上来
21. cut across 抄近路，走捷径
22. cut down（on）削减；降低
23. cut off 阻断；切断；使隔绝
24. drop by/in 顺便来访（无意的）
25. fall back on 求助于；转而依靠
26. fall behind 落后
27. fall in with 碰见；符合，与……一致
28. get across 解释清楚，使人了解
29. get along（with）有进展；生活得，过得
30. get at 够得着，触及；意思

是；理解
31. get away 离开，走开；逃脱
32. get by 混过；通过，经过
33. get down to 开始，着手（此处 to 为介词）；使失望
34. get in 进入；收回；收获
35. get out of 逃避；改掉
36. get rid of 除去；摆脱
37. get through 接通电话；度过（时间等）；结束，完成
38. get together 集合，聚集
39. give away 泄露；分送
40. give back 送还；恢复
41. give in 交上；投降，屈服
42. give up 停止，放弃
43. give way to 给……让路；对……让步（含屈服的意思）
44. go after 追求，求爱
45. go around/round 足够分配；流传
46. go by（时间等）过去；遵守，遵循
47. go in for 从事；追求；致力于；沉迷于
48. go into 研究，调查；进入
49. go over 复习，重温；（重复）检查，审查
50. go through 经历，经受（困难等）
51. hand in 交上，递交
52. hand out 散发；（平均）分发，发给
53. hold back 阻止，抑制
54. hold on 继续；不挂断；握住不放
55. keep on 保持；继续不断
56. keep up with 向……看齐；跟上
57. lay aside 把……搁置在一边；储蓄
58. lay off 休息；（临时）解雇
59. lay out 布置，安排；设计；制定
60. let alone 不干涉；更不用说
61. let down 放下，降低；使
62. live on（动物）以……为食；（人）靠……生活
63. look after 照顾，照料；注意，关心
64. look back 回头看；回顾；记忆
65. look down on/upon 看不起，轻视
66. look forward to 盼望，期待
67. look into 调查，观察
68. look out 留神，注意
69. look through 仔细查看；浏览；温习
70. make out 辨认出；理解

71. make up 组成，构成；捏造，编造；化妆；补充
72. pay back 偿还；回报
73. pay off 还清（债）；取得成功
74. pick out 选出；拣出
75. pick up 拾起；（车）中途搭（人）
76. pull in（车）停下；进站；（船）到岸
77. pull off 脱（帽、衣等）
78. pull on 对……有吸引力
79. put across/over 解释清楚，说明
80. put aside 储存，保留
81. put down 记下，放下；镇压；评定
82. put forward 提出
83. put off 推迟
84. put on 上演；（体重）增加；穿上，戴上
85. put out 熄灭；关（灯）
86. put up 建造，搭起；张贴；提（价）；提供食宿
87. run down 追捕；贬低；（逐渐）减少；（逐渐）变弱；撞倒，撞沉
88. run out（of）用完，耗尽
89. run through 游览；贯穿；普遍存在于
90. see off 给……送行
91. see to 注意；负责；照料；修理
92. set about 开始，着手；耗尽
93. set down 记下；记入；放下；卸下
94. set off 动身，出发；引起；使发生
95. set up 创立，建立；树立；资助
96. show off 卖弄，炫耀
97. stand by 支持；袖手旁观；做好准备
98. stand for 代表，意味着；支持；是……的缩写
99. take after（在外貌、性格等方面）与（父、母）相像
100. take…for 把……认为是，把……看成为
101. take off 起飞；脱下；匆匆离开
102. take over 接收，接管；借用；承袭
103. take to 对……产生好感；开始喜欢；开始从事
104. take up 开始从事；占去，占据
105. turn down 拒绝；关小，调低
106. turn out 结果是，（最后）

证明是；制造，生产；关掉

107. turn over 仔细考虑

108. turn to 变成；求助于，借助于

109. turn up 开大，调大；出现；来到

110. wait for 等候

111. wait on 服侍，侍候

112. watch out（for）密切注意，提防

113. wear out 穿破；磨损

114. wonder at 对……感到惊讶

115. work at 从事于，致力于

116. work out 算出；想出；制定出；解决

117. worry about（使）担心，（使）发愁

118. write down 写下；把……描写成

119. write off 注销；勾销；取消

120. yield to 屈服，服从

二、常用介词固定搭配

1. above all 最重要的是；尤其是
2. after all 毕竟；终究
3. ahead of 在……之前
4. ahead of time 提前
5. all at once 突然；同时，一起
6. all but 除了……都；几乎，差不多
7. all of a sudden 忽然，突然，出乎意料地
8. all over 到处，遍及
9. all over again 再一次，重新
10. all the same 仍然，照样地
11. all the time 一直，始终
12. and so on/fort 诸如此类，等等
13. anything but 根本不，除……以外任何事情
14. apart from 除……以外（别无，尚有）
15. as a matter of fact 事实上，其实
16. as a result 因此，作为结果
17. as a result of 作为……的结果，由于
18. as a rule 通常，多半，照例
19. as for/to 至于，关于
20. as usual 像往常一样，照例
21. aside from 除了……以外（尚有）
22. at a loss 不知所措，困惑；亏本地
23. at all costs 不惜任何代价，无论如何
24. at all events 无论如何，不管怎样

25. at any rate 无论如何；至少
26. at best 充其量，至多
27. at first 起先，最初
28. at first sight 乍一看，初看起来
29. at hand 近在手边；在附近
30. at heart 在内心里；本质上
31. at intervals 不时；每隔……时间/距离
32. at large 自由行动的；详尽的；一般的
33. at last 终于
34. at least 至少；无论如何
35. at length 最后，终于；详细地
36. at most 至多，不超过
37. at no time 从不；决不
38. at once 立刻，马上；同时，一起
39. at one time 同时；曾经；一度
40. at present 现在，目前
41. at sb. /sb.'s disposal 由某人支配；供……使用
42. at the cost of 以……为代价
43. at the same time 同时；然而，不过
44. at this rate 照此速度；照这样下去
45. at times 有时，不时，间或
46. back and forth 来回地，反复地
47. because of 因为，由于
48. before long 不久（以后）
49. beside the point 离题；不中肯；不相干的
50. beyond question 毫无疑问，确定无疑
51. by accident 偶然
52. by air 通过航空途径
53. by all means 尽一切办法；一定，务必
54. by chance 偶然；意外地，碰巧
55. by means of 用；依靠
56. by mistake 错误地；无意中（做了某件错事）
57. by no means 决不；并没有
58. by reason of 由于，因为
59. by the way 顺便地；附带说说
60. by/in virtue of 依靠……（的力量）；由于
61. by way of 通过……方法/形式；经过，经由
62. for ever 永远；永久地
63. for good 永久地；决定性地
64. for instance 例如，比如
65. for the better 好转，向好的方向发展

66. for the moment/present 暂时；目前
67. for the sake of 为了，为了……的利益
68. for the time being 暂时；眼下
69. from time to time 有时；不时
70. from now on 今后，从今以后
71. in a hurry 匆忙；很快地；急于
72. in a moment 立即，马上
73. in a sense 从某种意义上说
74. in a/one way 从某一点上看；在某种程度上
75. in a/one word 简言之，总之，一句话
76. in accordance with 与……一致；按照，依据
77. in addition 另外，加之
78. in addition to 除……之外（还）
79. in advance 预先，事先
80. in all 总共，合计
81. in any case 无论如何；总之
82. in brief 简言之；以简洁的形式
83. in case of 假使……，如果发生……；防备
84. in charge of 主管，负责
85. in common 共用的；共有的
86. in consequence of 结果，因此
87. in debt 欠债，欠情
88. in detail 详细地
89. in difficulty 处境困难
90. in effect 实际上；事实上
91. in favor of 赞同……，支持……
92. in future 今后，从今以后
93. in general 一般来说；大体上
94. in hand（工作等）正在进行中；待办理
95. in honor of 向……表示敬意；为纪念
96. in itself 本质上；就其本身而言
97. in line with 跟……一致；符合
98. in memory of 以纪念……，为了纪念……
99. in no case 决不，无论如何不
100. in no way 一点也不；决不
101. in order to 为了……，以……为目的
102. in other words 也就是说，换句话说
103. in part 在某种程度上；部分地
104. in particular 特别地；尤其
105. in place 在合适的位置；

适当的；相称的
106. in place of 代替，取代，交换
107. in practice 在实践中；在不断练习中
108. in proportion to 与……成比例；与……相称
109. in quantity（= in large quantities）大量
110. in question 正被谈论的
111. in relation to 关于，涉及，有关；与……相比
112. in return 作为报答；作为回报
113. in return for 作为……的交换；作为……的报答
114. in short 总之，简言之
115. in sight of 被见到；看得见；在望，在即
116. in spite of 不管，不顾
117. in step 步调一致地；合拍
118. in step with 与……合步调，与……步调一致
119. in tears 流着泪；含着泪；哭着
120. in the course of 在……期间；在……过程中
121. in the distance 在远处
122. in the end 最后；终于
123. in the event of 如果……发生，万一
124. in the face of 面对；即使
125. in the first place 首先，第一点
126. in the future 将来
127. in the least 一点儿，丝毫
128. in the light of 鉴于，由于；按照，根据
129. in the way 挡道的，妨碍人的，使人不便的
130. in the world 到底，究竟
131. in time 及时；最后；终于
132. in touch 联系，接触
133. in touch with 与……有联系；有……的消息
134. in turn 依次，轮流；反过来
135. in vain 徒劳，白辛苦；不尊敬地
136. instead of 代替；而不是……
137. more or less 或多或少；左右；有点儿
138. no doubt 无疑地
139. no longer 不再
140. no more 不再；不再存在；也不
141. now and then 时而，不时，偶尔
142. of course 当然，自然
143. on and off 有时；断断续

续地；间歇地

144. off duty 下班
145. on a large scale 大规模地
146. on a small scale 小规模地
147. on account of 因为，由于
148. on the average 平均而言；通常
149. on behalf of 代表……；为了……
150. on board 在船（车、飞机）上
151. on business 因事，因公
152. on condition that 如果……；在……条件下
153. on duty 值班，当班
154. on earth 究竟；到底；在世界上
155. on fire 起火，着火
156. on foot 步行；在进行中
157. on guard 站岗；值班
158. on hand 现有；在手头；在场；到场
159. on occasions 间或，有时
160. on one's guard 警惕；提防
161. on one's own 独自地；独立地
162. on purpose 有意，故意地
163. on sale 出售；上市；廉价出售
164. on schedule 按时间表；准时
165. on second thoughts 进一步考虑后；继而一想
166. on the contrary 正相反
167. on the grounds of 以……为理由，根据
168. on the one hand 一方面
169. on the other hand 另一方面
170. on/upon the point of 即将……之时，正要……的时候
171. on the road 在旅途中；（to）在……过程
172. on the side 作为兼职；另外
173. on/upon the spot 立即；在现场
174. on the whole 总地看来；大体上
175. once for all 一劳永逸地；永远地
176. once in a while 偶尔，间或
177. once more/again 再一次
178. once upon a time（常用于故事开头）从前
179. out of breath 上气不接下气
180. out of control 失去控制
181. out of date 过时的；废弃的
182. out of order 不整齐；（工作）不正常的；出故障的
183. out of place 不在合适的位

置；不恰当的

184. out of practice 荒疏；久不练习

185. out of sight 看不见；在视程之外

186. out of the question 办不到的；不可能的；不必谈的

187. out of touch（with）与……失去联系；没有……的消息

188. over and over（again）反复，再三

189. so as to 为的是；结果是……；以致

190. so…as to 如此……以致

191. so far 迄今为止；就此说来

192. so/as far as … be concern 就……而言

193. sooner or later 迟早，早晚

194. thanks to 幸亏；由于

三、常用名词固定搭配

1. absence from 缺席；离开
2. have access to 可以接近；可以利用
3. make the acquaintance of sb. 结识某人
4. have a nodding acquaintance with 与……有点头之交
5. take action 采取行动
6. admission to 准许
7. take advantage of 利用；趁……之机
8. make an agreement with 与……达成协议
9. make/offer an apology to sb. 向某人道歉
10. make an appeal to sb. 向某人发出呼吁
11. application for 申请
12. make an appointment with sb. 与某人约会
13. approach to 通往……的方法；接近
14. come to sb.'s assistance 帮助某人
15. make an attempt to do sth. 试图做某事
16. pay attention to 注意
17. have an authority over 对……有（行使）权利
18. keep one's balance 保持（身体）平衡
19. set up a barrier between 在……中间设置障碍
20. belief in 相信
21. do/try one's best 努力，尽力
22. make the best of 充分利用
23. catch one's breath 喘气
24. take care of 爱护；照料
25. give a challenge 挑战

26. rise to the challenge 接受挑战
27. take a chance 冒险；投机
28. take charge of 管理，接管
29. lay a claim 要求；主张；自以为
30. set up a claim to sth. 提出对某事物的要求
31. combination with 与……结合
32. seek comfort in 在……中寻找安慰
33. take comfort in 在……中得到安慰
34. get command of 控制
35. take command of 开始担任……的指挥
36. communication with 与……通信；与……交流
37. keep company with 和……结交；和……亲热
38. keep sb. company 陪伴某人；陪某人同走
39. make a comparison between 把……进行比较
40. competition with/against 与某人竞争
41. keep competition between 在……之间进行竞争
42. complaint about/of 对……抱怨
43. make a complaint against 控告
44. come to a conclusion 得出结论
45. have confidence in sb. 信任某人
46. leave sth. out of consideration 对某事不加考虑
47. take into consideration 考虑到
48. be in contact with 与……接触
49. be out of contact with 与……失去联系
50. have contact with 和……接触
51. lose contact with 与……失去联系
52. present a striking contrast between 使两者形成鲜明的对照
53. have control over/of 对……控制
54. lose control of 失去对……控制
55. have/ hold a conversation with 与……谈话
56. commit a crime 犯罪
57. arouse sb. 's curiosity about sth. 激起某人对某事物的好奇心
58. lay a curse upon sb. 诅咒某人
59. do damage to 损害……
60. come to a decision 决定下来
61. arrive at a decision 决定下来
62. make a decision 作决定
63. take a delight in 以……为乐

64. take delivery of 提取
65. take one's departure 动身，出发
66. give a description of 描写
67. drive sb. to despair 使某人陷入绝望
68. have the determination to do 决心干……
69. make a difference between 区别对待
70. make a difference to 使……产生变化
71. have difficulty in doing sth. 做某事有困难
72. draw a clear distinction between 分清
73. come into effect 生效；实施
74. put into effect 实行；使生效，使起作用
75. take effect 生效，起作用
76. put emphasis on/upon 着重于，把重点放在
77. make one's entrance 进入
78. make an error 犯错误
79. give evidence of 有……迹象
80. set a good example to sb. 为某人树立榜样
81. make no exceptions 不容许有例外
82. catch sb.'s eye 引人注目
83. keep an eye on 留意，照看
84. have faith in 对……信任
85. lose faith in 失去对……信任
86. keep faith 忠于信仰
87. farewell to 对……永别了；不会再……
88. make one's farewell 道别，告辞
89. come into fashion 开始风行
90. follow the fashion 赶时髦
91. make fashion 做样子
92. set the fashion 创立新式样
93. find fault (with) 抱怨，找茬
94. catch fire 着火
95. set fire to 使燃烧，点燃
96. come into a fortune 继承一笔财产
97. make a fortune 发财
98. try one's fortune 碰运气
99. make friends (with) 交朋友
100. make fun of 取笑，嘲笑
101. give/take a glance at 对……粗略地看一下
102. catch/get a glimpse of 瞥见
103. come to a halt 停止
104. do sb. harm 损害某人
105. keep one's head 保持镇定
106. lose one's head 仓皇失措，慌乱
107. learn by heart 背诵，记住
108. lose heart 失去勇气，丧失

信心
109. get hold of 抓住；得到
110. hunger for/after 渴望
111. attach importance 重视
112. have an influence on/upon 对……有影响
113. make inquiries of sb. about sth. 向某人询问某事
114. hold an inquiry into sth. 对某事进行调查
115. play a joke on sb. 开某人的玩笑
116. come to sb.'s knowledge 被某人知道
117. throw light on/upon 阐明某事，使人了解某事
118. fall in love with 爱上
119. make mention of 提及……
120. have mercy on/upon 对……表示怜悯
121. bring/call to mind 想起
122. have sth. in mind 记得，想到
123. keep/bear in mind 记住
124. make up one's mind 下决心，决意
125. keep one's mind on 专注于
126. make the most of 充分利用
127. come to sb.'s notice 引起某人的注意
128. take notice of 注意到
129. make/take an objection to 对……表示反对
130. obstacle to 成为……的障碍
131. bring/put into operation 手术；操作；运转；运算
132. come/go into operation 实行；生效
133. place an order for sth. with 向……订购某物
134. keep pace with 与……并驾齐驱；共同前进
135. take pains 努力，尽力；煞费苦心
136. play a part (in) (在……中) 扮演角色；参与
137. take part in 参加
138. take place 发生；进行；举行
139. take the place of 取代，代替
140. come to a point 变尖锐；到紧要关头
141. keep to the point 扣住主题
142. make a point 立论，证明论点
143. hold the position of (as) 担任……职务
144. come into possession of sth. 占有某物
145. take possession of 占有；占领
146. make a practice of 经常进行

147. put in/into practice 实施，实行
148. have a preference for 偏爱……
149. have a prejudice against sb. 对某人有偏见
150. make preparations for 为……做准备
151. take pride in 以……自豪，对……感到得意
152. enjoy privileges 享受特权
153. grant sb. the privilege of doing 赋予某人做……的权利
154. make a promise 许下诺言
155. keep a promise 遵守诺言
156. carry out a promise 履行诺言
157. break a promise 不遵守诺言
158. recovery from 从……中恢复
159. make a reduction 减小，缩小
160. make reference to 提到
161. have no reference to 与……无关
162. give one's regards to sb. 向某人致意
163. make/offer resistance to 对……抵抗
164. take the resolution 决心干某事
165. have resort to sb. 求助于某人
166. make a response 对……做出响应
167. take the responsibility for 负起对某事的责任
168. get/take a rise out of sb. 惹得某人恼怒
169. give rise to 引起；使发生
170. run/take a risk 冒险
171. play a role in 在……中扮演角色（起作用）
172. express one's satisfaction at/with 对……表示满意
173. make satisfaction for 赔偿，补偿
174. throw a scare into sb. 吓坏某人
175. come to one's senses 苏醒过来；恢复理性
176. make sense 讲得通；言之有理
177. throw/cast/put into the shade 使逊色，使相形见绌
178. cast a shadow over 蒙上阴影
179. catch at shadows 捕风捉影
180. put sb. to shame 羞辱某人
181. do one's share for sth. 为……贡献一份力量
182. go shares 合伙经营；分享；分担
183. take/bear one's share of 承担一份

184. catch sight of 看见，发现
185. lose sight of 看不见，在视野之外
186. take the firm stand 站稳立场
187. take a stand for/against sth. 表示赞成/反对某事
188. follow/tread in sb's step 踏着某人的足迹；效仿
189. take stock 清查存货，盘存
190. take stock in 购买（公司）；相信
191. take stock of 估量，观察
192. lay/place/put stress on/upon 把重点放在……上
193. substitute for sth. 替代某物
194. express sympathy for/with sb. 对某人表示慰问
195. have a talk with sb. 与某人交谈
196. make talk 闲谈
197. get/go into a temper 发脾气
198. lose one's temper 发脾气
199. have/run a temperature 发烧
200. take one's temperature 量体温
201. fall into temptation 受诱惑
202. resist temptation 抵制诱惑
203. give/yield way to tempt at 受诱惑
204. have a terror of sth. 感到恐怖
205. thanks to 由于；多亏
206. no thanks to 并非由于
207. do a threat to 对……形成威胁
208. take one's time 不着急，不慌忙
209. keep in touch with sb. 与某人保持联系
210. keep track of 记录；保持与……联系
211. lose track of 失去……的线索
212. set a trap 设陷阱
213. play a trick on sb. 捉弄某人
214. get into trouble 陷入困境，招致不幸
215. make trouble 闹事，捣乱
216. have trouble with 同……闹纠纷
217. make use of 使用，利用
218. put to use 使用
219. give way to 让路，让步
220. lead the way 带路，引路
221. make way 让路，腾出地方/位置
222. keep one's word 守信用

附录二　作文六种常用句式表

	常用句式
原因	1. The answer to this problem involves many factors. 2. Perhaps the primary factor is that… 3. One of the most common factors (causes) is that… 4. The most important aspect is that… 5. The change in…largely results from the fact that… 6. A number of factors are accountable for this situation. 7. We may blame…, but the real causes are… 8. But the essential cause is that…
比较	1. The advantage far outweighs the disadvantages. 2. A and B differ in several ways. 3. For all the disadvantages, it has its compensating advantages. 4. It is true that…, but the chief faults are… 5. It is reasonable to maintain that…but it would be foolish to claim that. 6. A may be preferable to…, but A suffers from the disadvantages that… 7. However, the same is not applicable to… 8. Evidently, it has both negative and positive effects. 9. It is quite different from… 10. From the contrary, we can see that… 11. The same is true of… 12. People used to think…, but things are different now. 13. A and B has several points in common. 14. The advantages of A are much greater than those of B. 15. Like anything else, it has its faults. 16. Wondering as A is, it has its drawbacks. 17. …is better than…But…also have its own disadvantages. 18. The common things between them is…

续表

	常用句式
批驳	1. There is a grain of truth in these statements, but they ignore a more important fact. 2. Some people say…, but it does not hold… 3. Many of us have been under the illusion that… 4. It makes no sense to argue for… 5. Such a statement mainly rests on the assumption that… 6. Contrary to what is widely accepted, I maintain that… 7. Too much stress placed on…may lead to… 8. It is true that…, but one vital point is being left out. 9. A close examination would reveal how ridiculous the statement is. 10. More and more people begin to argue that… 11. The argument of…has become more seriously.
举例	1. A good case in point is… 2. As an illustration, we may take… 3. …is often cited as an example. 4. Such examples might be given easily. 5. Take…for an example. 6. For instance… 7. There is a good illustration about…
结果	1. Its consequence can be so great that… 2. The immediate result it produces is… 3. It may give rise to a host of problems. 4. It will exercise a profound influence upon… 5. On the consequence, … 6. The problems arouse quite a number of… 7. As a result… 8. The results bought…

续表

	常用句式
证明	1. No one can deny the fact that… 2. There is sufficient evidence to show that… 3. Unfortunately, none of the available data shows… 4. His idea is hardly supported by facts. 5. According to statistics proved by…, it can be seen that… 6. Recent studies indicate that… 7. It is proved that…

附录三　常用衔接词汇表

一、逻辑

因果关系	as a result/as a result of 结果 on account of 由于 accordingly 因此 therefore 因此 because of 由于 so that 因此 due to 由于 consequently 因此；结果 owing to 由于 hence 因此 thanks to 多亏 now that 既然 since 自……以来；既然
解释关系	as a matter of that 大约，大概 in this case 既然这样 as well 倒不如，还是……的好 frankly speaking 坦白地讲
推理关系	if so 假如这样的话 that implies 意味着 or else 否则 under no circumstances 在这种情况下 otherwise 否则
递进关系	in other words 换句话说 what's more 另外 last but not least 最后的但并非最不重要的 that is to say 也就是说 besides 还有，另外 in addition 另外 additionally 又 furthermore 此外，而且

续表

比较关系	equally 相等的；公平的 in cooperation with 与……相比 on the contrary 相反地 in contrast 相反 while 虽然 in the same way 同样地 instead 更换，替代
选择关系	not…but 不是……而是 neither…nor 既不是……也不是 instead…of 替代 alternatively 二者选一的 rather than 胜于 either…or 或者是……
转折关系	although 尽管 though 虽然，可是 despite 虽然 otherwise 另外，否则 at the same time 同时 yet 仍，然而，但是 even though 甚至 however 但是，然而 nevertheless 然而 regardless of 不管，不顾 notwithstanding 虽然，尽管 still 尽管如此
总结关系	all in all/in all/in sum/in a word 总而言之 briefly 简要地 in terms 在……中 in conclusion/to conclusion 总之 in summary/to summarize 总之，简要

续表

顺序关系	first/firstly/first of all 第一，首先 eventually/lastly/in the end/finally 最后 afterwards 后来的 above all 首先 furthermore 接着
强调关系	most important 最重要的 of course 当然 with great emphasis on 强调的是 indeed 的确
过渡关系	as regards/concerning/regarding/as to/as for 关于，至于 by the way 顺便的 with reference to 关于 talking of 谈到 incidentally 顺便提到
举例关系	as follows 如下 a case in point 一个恰当的例子 for example/for instance 例如 to illustrate 举例说明 including 包括
指代关系	that is/that is to say 也就是说
时间关系	after a while 过一会 meanwhile 同时 afterwards 然后 until now 到现在为止 as long as 只要，在……的时候 thereafter 从那时以后 at last/at length/in the past 最后

二、承上启下

起始	at first 最初 on the whole 总体来说 recently 最近 it goes without saying that…不用说 lately 最近 in general 一般来说 to start with 首先，第一 to begin with 首先 on one hand…on the other hand…一方面……另一方面…… first/firstly/in the beginning 第一 for one thing…for another thing… 首先……其次……
承接	also/too 并且，又 such as 正如 at any rate 无论如何 truly 事实上；真正的 after a while 过了一会 no doubt 无疑地 moreover 而且此外 of course 当然 incidentally 顺便提一句 then 然后 what is more 而且，此外 still 仍然 later 后来 in fact 事实上 by this time 此时 so 所以 besides 此外 second/secondly 第二 similarly 同样地 third/thirdly 第三

续表

承接	soon 不久 unlikely 不像…… for another 其次 in addition 此外 in addition to 除……之外
转折	in fact/as a matter of 事实上 despite 尽管；虽然 but 但是 especially 特别的 anyway 无论如何 fortunately 幸运地 by this time 此时 however 无论如何 nonetheless 尽管如此 in spite of 虽然，尽管 conversely 相反地 nevertheless 不过，仍然 all the time 依然，照样 no doubt 无疑地 after all 毕竟 notwithstanding 虽然 whereas 然而 yet 然而，但是
总结	above all 最重要的是 in a word/in sum/in summary 总之 accordingly 于是 therefore 因此 as a consequence 因此 thus 因此 as a result 结果 to speak frankly 坦白地说

续表

总结	in short 简而言之 all in all 总之 hence 因此 to sum up/to summarize 简而言之 eventually 最后 undoubtedly 毫无疑问 finally 最后 to conclude 总而言之 by and large 一般来说 surely 无疑 as has been noted 如前所述 as I have said 如我所说

附录四 常用谚语和格言表

常用汉英谚语	1. No competition, no progress. 没有竞争就没有进步。 2. God helps those who help themselves. 天助自助者。 3. Easier said than done. 说起来容易做起来难。 4. Where there is a will, there is a way. 有志者事竟成。 5. One false step will make a great difference. 失之毫厘，谬之千里。 6. Slow and steady wins the race. 稳扎稳打无往而不胜。 7. A fall into the pit, a gain in your wit. 吃一堑，长一智。 8. Experience is the mother of wisdom. 实践出真理。 9. A famed person and a fattened pig are alike in danger. 人怕出名猪怕壮。 10. Beauty without virtue is a rose without fragrance. 无德之美犹如没有香味的玫瑰，徒有其表。 11. More hasty, less speed. 欲速则不达。 12. It's never too old to learn. 活到老，学到老。 13. All that glitters is not gold. 闪光的未必都是金子。 14. A journey of a thousand miles begins with a single step. 千里之行始于足下。 15. Look before you leap. 三思而后行。 16. Rome was not built in a day. 伟业非一日之功。 17. Great minds think alike. 英雄所见略同。 18. Well begun, half done. 好的开始等于成功的一半。 19. It is hard to please all. 众口难调。 20. Out of sight, out of mind. 眼不见，心不念。 21. Facts speak plainer than words. 事实胜于雄辩。 22. Call black white and white black. 颠倒黑白。 23. First things first. 凡事有轻重缓急。 24. Ill news travels fast. 坏事传千里。

续表

常用汉英谚语	25. A friend in need is a friend indeed. 患难见真情。 26. Live not to eat, but eat to live. 活着不是为了吃饭，吃饭是为了活着。 27. Action speaks louder than words. 行动胜过语言。 28. East or west, home is the best. 金窝银窝不如自家草窝。 29. It's not the gay coat that makes the gentleman. 君子在德不在衣。 30. Beauty will buy no beef. 漂亮不能当饭吃。 31. Like and like make good friends. 趣味相投。 32. The older, the wiser. 姜是老的辣。 33. Do as Romans do in Rome. 入乡随俗。 34. An idle youth, a needy age. 少壮不努力，老大徒伤悲。 35. As the tree, so the fruit. 种瓜得瓜，种豆得豆。 36. To live is to learn; to learn is to better live. 活着为了学习，学习为了更好地活着。 37. Practice makes perfect. 熟能生巧。 38. All work and no play make jack a dull boy. 只工作不休息，聪明孩子也变傻。 39. He lives long that lives well. 活得好等于活得久。 40. A brother is a friend given by god. 兄弟是天赐的朋友。 41. All things are difficult before they are easy. 万事开头难。 42. Where there is life, there is hope. 留得青山在，不怕没柴烧。 43. A friend is known till needed. 路遥知马力，日久见人心。 44. As you make your bed, so you must live in it. 自作自受。 45. A good name is better than riches. 美名胜财富。 46. As they brew, so let them drink. 自作自受。 47. A good beginning makes a good ending. 善始才有善终。 48. Bad news has wings. 好事不出门，恶事传千里。 49. Company in distress makes trouble less. 同病相怜，同忧相救。 50. Call a spade a spade. 直言不讳。 51. Birds of a feather flock together 物以类聚，人以群分。

续表

常用汉英谚语	52. Constant dripping wears away the stone. 滴水石穿。 53. Don't teach fish to swim. 不要班门弄斧。 54. Easy come, easy go. 易得则易失。 55. Every dog has his day. 每个人都有得意的一天。 56. Every why has a wherefore. 凡事均有因。 57. God helps those who help themselves. 苍天不负苦心人。 58. Laugh and grow fat. 心宽体胖。 59. Misfortune tell us what fortune is. 不经灾难不知福。 60. Nothing seek, nothing find. 无所求则无所获。 61. One man's meat is another man's poison. 萝卜青菜，各有所爱。 62. Time is money. 时间就是金钱。 63. Tastes differ. 口味各不相同。 64. The biter is sometimes bit. 害人反害己。 65. The course of true love never did run smooth. 好事多磨。 66. Time and tide wait for no man. 岁月不饶人。 67. There is no smoke without fire. 无风不起浪。 68. The early bird catches the worm. 早起的鸟儿有虫吃。 69. Time lost cannot be won again. 岁月一去不复返。 70. Two's company, three's none. 两人成伴，三人不欢。 71. Constant dripping wears away the stone. 锲而不舍，金石可镂。 72. Get back on the roundabouts. 失之东隅，收之桑榆。 73. The shortest answer is doing. 最简短的回答就是行动。 74. What's done cannot be undone. 覆水难收。 75. Hunger is the best sauce. 饥饿是最好的调味品。 76. Four short words sum up what has lifted most successful individuals above the crowd: a little bit more. 成功的秘诀就是四个简单的字：多一点点。 77. It never rains but it pours. 祸不单行。 78. In doing we learn. 经一事，长一智。

续表

常用汉英谚语	79. Let's cross the bridge when we come to it. 船到桥头自然直。 80. Keeping is harder than winning. 创业不易，守业更难。 81. Stick to it, and you'll succeed. 只要人有恒，万事都能成。 82. Light come, light go. 来得容易，去得快。 83. It is good to learn at another man's cost. 前车之鉴。 84. We must not lie down, and cry, "God help us." 求神不如求己。 85. A plant may produce new flowers; man is young but once. 花有重开日，人无再少年。 86. What may be done at any time will be done at no time. 明日待明日，明日不再来。 87. Take care of the pence, and the pounds will take care of themselves. 积少自然成多。 88. No man is wise at all times. 智者千虑，必有一失。 89. An ounce of prevention is worth a pound of cure. 一分预防胜似十分治疗。 90. Industry is fortune's right hand, and frugality her left. 勤勉是幸运的右手，节约是幸运的左手。 91. He who laughs last laughs best. 谁笑在最后，谁笑得最好。 92. No man is born wise or learned. 人非生而知之。 93. Courage and resolution are the spirit and soul of virtue. 勇敢和坚决是美德的灵魂。 94. Life is full of ups and downs. 生活充满起伏。 95. To err is human. 人非圣贤，孰能无过。 96. There are tricks in every trade. 行行有窍门，事事有秘诀。 97. What must be must be. 要尊重客观规律。 98. Zeal without knowledge is a runaway horse. 无知的狂热如同脱缰之马。

续表

<table>
<tr><td>常用
英汉
格言</td><td>1. Human pride is human weakness.
骄傲乃人类之弱点。
—— M. B. Eddy 艾迪
2. Fate chooses your relatives, you choose your friends.
亲戚乃命定，朋友靠选择。
—— Abbe Jacques Delille 德力尔
3. Gods determine what you're going to be.
人生的奋斗目标决定你将成为什么样的人。
—— Julius Eriving 欧文
4. An aim in life is the only fortune worth finding.
生活的目标，是唯一值得寻找的财富。
—— Robert Liuris Stevenson 史蒂文森
5. What makes life dreary is the want of motive.
没有了目的，生活便郁闷无光。
—— George Eliot 乔治・埃略特
6. If winter comes, can spring be far behind?
冬天来了，春天还会远吗？
——Shelley 雪莱
7. There is no royal road to learning.
学问之路无捷径。
—— Trollop 特勒普
8. The first step to knowledge is to know that we are ignorant.
获得知识的第一步是要知道自己无知。
—— Cecil 塞西尔
9. Politeness costs nothing and gains everything.
礼貌无须花钱，却能赢得一切。
—— M. W. Montague 蒙塔古
10. Nothing in life is to be feared. It is only to be understood.
生活中没有什么可怕的东西，只有需要理解的东西。
—— Marie Curie 居里夫人</td></tr>
</table>

续表

<table>
<tr><td>常用英汉格言</td><td>11. Try not to become a man of success but rather try to become a man of value.
不要为做一个成功的人而努力，而要为做一个有价值的人而努力。
——A. Einstein 爱因斯坦
12. You have to believe in yourself. That is the secret of success.
人必须要有自信，这是成功的秘密。
——Charles Chaplin 卓别林
13. Victory won't come to me unless I go to it.
胜利不会向我们走来的，我必须走向胜利。
—— M. Moore 穆尔
14. Man errs as long as he strives.
失误是进取的代价。
——Goethe 歌德
15. He who seize the right moment, is the right man.
谁把握机遇，谁就心想事成。
——Goethe 歌德
16. Self-trust is the first secret of success.
自信乃成功之第一秘诀。
—— R. Emerson 爱默生
17. Speech is silver, but silence is gold.
雄辩是银，沉默是金。
—— T. Carlyle 卡莱尔
18. The brighter you are, the more you have to learn.
越聪明的人，越需要学习。
—— D. Herald 赫罗尔德
19. The darkest hour is that before the dawn.
黎明前的时分是最黑暗的。
—— Fuller 富勒
20. The man who has made up his mind to win will never say "impossible".
凡是决心取得胜利的人是从来不说“不可能”的。
—— Bonaparte Napoleon 拿破仑</td></tr>
</table>

续表

常用英汉格言	21. Lookers-on see most of the game. 旁观者清。 —— Smedley 斯密莱
	22. Knowledge is a treasure, but practice is the key to it. 知识是一座宝库，而实践就是开启宝库的钥匙。 —— Fuller 富勒
	23. It is better to be faithful than famous. 守信用胜过有名气。 —— T. Roosevelt 罗斯福
	24. Knowledge is power. 知识就是力量。 —— F. Bacon 培根
	25. A strong man will struggle with a storms of fate. 强者能同命运的风暴抗争。 ——Thomas Edition 爱迪生
	26. Energy and persistence conquer all things. 能量加毅力可以征服一切。 —— Benjamin Franklin 富兰克林
	27. Cease to struggle and you cease to live. 生命不止，奋斗不息。 —— Thomas Carlyle 卡莱尔
	28. Living without an aim is like sailing without a compass. 生活没有目标，犹如航海没有罗盘。 —— John Ruskin 罗斯金
	29. There is no such thing as a great talent without great will. 没有伟大的意志力，便没有雄才大略。 ——Balzac 巴尔扎克
	30. We must accept finite disappointment, but we must never lose infinite hope. 我们必须接受失望，因为它是有限的，但千万不可以失去希望，因为它是无穷的。 —— Mattin Luther King 马丁·路德·金

续表

常用英汉格言	31. The people who get on in this world are the people who get up and look for circumstances they want, and if they cannot find them, make them. 在这个世界上取得成功的人，都努力去寻找他们想要的机会，如果找不到机会，他们便自己创造机会。 ——Bernara Shaw 萧伯纳
	32. I think success has no rules, but you can learn a lot from failure. 成功没有定律，但你可从失败中找到这些定律。 ——Jean Kerr 珍妮·克儿
	33. There are no secrets to success. It is the result of preparation, hard work, and learning from failure. 成功没有什么秘诀。它只是准备、勤劳以及从失败中找答案的结果。 ——Colin L. Powell 克林·鲍威尔
	34. Behind every successful man there's a lot of unsuccessful years. 每位成功者的背后都有很多不成功的岁月。 ——Bob Brown 博比·布朗

附录五　图表中“data”的具体表达法

一、data 在不同情况下的表达

增加：increase/raise/rise/go up

减少：decrease/grow down/drop/fall

波动：fluctuate/rebound/undulate/wave

稳定：remain stable/stabilize/level off

达到：come to/reach/jump to

多达，高达：up to/as many as/as high as/peak at

共计：to account to/to add to/to cover to

data 在某一个时间段固定不变：fixed in time

在一系列的时间段中转变：changes over time

二、表示倍数

比……多一倍：... as many/much again as .../... is twice (times) as much as .../... is twice (times) the amount of.../... is doubled.../...increase two times as...

三、最常见的表达法

（1）The number of... + increase/jump/rise/decrease/drop/fall/fluctuate ... + insignificantly/significantly/slightly/suddenly/rapidly/dramatically/sharply/steeply/steadily/gradually/slowly... + from（第一时间）to（第二时间）/between（第一时间）and（第二时间）

（2）There was a（very）sudden/rapid/dramatic/significant/sharp/steep/steady/gradual/slow/slight ... + increase/jump/rise/

decrease/drop/fall… + in the number of…from（第一时间）to（第二时间）/between（第一时间）and（第二时间）

四、描述稳定的数据

The number of…remained steady/stable from（第一时间）to（第二时间）/between（第一时间）and（第二时间）

The number of…stayed the same from（第一时间）to（第二时间）/between（第一时间）and（第二时间）

There was little change/hardly any change/no change in the number of…from from（第一时间）to（第二时间）/between（第一时间）and（第二时间）

五、描述不同状态的数据

表示高点极值：The monthly profit/The figures/The situation… + peaked in（月/年）<具体的时间点用 at/at…%

或者 reached a peak/a high point at…%/…（极点 data）

表示低点极值：…bottomed out/reached/ + the bottom/a low point

表示平均值：to have an average of

最大、小值：maximum/minimum

六、最常用的固定搭配

并列：as well as（句首/中），also，as well（句尾），either，neither，too，moreover，furthermore，in addition，additionally，besides，what's more，apart from…

举例：for example，for instance，to illustrate，as an illustration，in particular，particularly，especially…

事实：as a matter of fact，in fact，actually，as long as，so long

as…

相似：similarly，likewise（句首/尾），at the same time，equally…

转折：however，whereas，nevertheless，nonetheless，though，although，even though，while，yet，on the contrary，contrarily，in contrast，conversely，on the other hand，unlikely，in stead（of），in spite of，despite of…

相反：contrary to，conversely…

比较：to be a contrast to 与……成对照；by contrast with 和……比起来；for the sake of comparison 为比较可见；in contrast with/to 和……形成对比；to comparewith 把……与比较（相同点）；to contrast…with 把……与比较（不同点）；be superior/inferior to…比……好（差）……

七、表示比例

（1）to be direct/inverse proportion（rate）to

与……成正比/反比

（2）to be in a ratio of A to B

比例为 A 比 B

（3）the proportion of A to B is X to Y

A 和 B 的比例为 X 比 Y

（4）to be proportionate/propotional to

（与……）成比例

（5）to be out of proportion（to）

（与……）不成比例

八、表示不确定的数据

大约：about，around，some，more or less，approximately，

roughly，in the neighborhood of…

少于：fewer，fewer than，less than，within，below，under…

差不多：more or less，almost，close on，nearly，towards…

多于：more than，over，above，upwards of，add…

表示范围：from…to…，between…and…，for…to…（多长时间直到）

相邻的数：one or two（一两个），by twos and threes（三三两两）

“数十，数百，数千”：ten/dozen/score/hundred/thousand/million/billion + of + 名词复数